TRACING YOUR
TEXTILE ANCESTORS

D1471046

TRACING YOUR TEXTILE ANCESTORS

VIVIEN TEASDALE

Pen & Sword
FAMILY HISTORY

First published in Great Britain in 2009 by
PEN & SWORD FAMILY HISTORY
an imprint of
Pen & Sword Books Ltd
47 Church Street
Barnsley
South Yorkshire
S70 2AS

ISBN 978 1 84415 870 6

A CIP catalogue record for this book is available from the British Library

Printed and bound in England by
CPI UK

Pen & Sword Books Ltd incorporates the Imprints of
Pen & Sword Aviation, Pen & Sword Family History, Pen & Sword Maritime,
Pen & Sword Military, Wharncliffe Local History, Pen & Sword Select,
Pen & Sword Military Classics, Leo Cooper, Remember When,
Seaforth Publishing and Frontline Publishing

For a complete list of Pen & Sword titles please contact
PEN & SWORD BOOKS LIMITED
47 Church Street, Barnsley, South Yorkshire, S70 2AS, England
E-mail: enquiries@pen-and-sword.co.uk
www.pen-and-sword.co.uk

CONTENTS

ACKNOWLEDGEMENTS

Any book of this nature requires a great deal of research, which involves visits to and correspondence with many libraries and archives. My thanks must go to every archive and record office in England and Wales that sent me information about the extent of their records. I then had the hard task of having to edit some of them. Many universities hold special collections, primarily for the purposes of academic research, but here too the archivists willingly gave me details of what might be of benefit to family historians. I have made particular use of my local libraries at Leeds, Wakefield, Manchester and Huddersfield (including the University of Huddersfield library and archives), where staff have, as always, been extremely helpful.

Over the years I have visited many museums, all of which seem to have improved unbelievably since the dry, glass-showcase days, with staff who are always friendly and obliging. Particularly I must mention the staff at Macclesfield silk mill, who gave me a guided tour and, with endless patience, explained the intricacies of the machinery on view. My thanks to all the museum staff that took the trouble to provide information and generally made my visits pleasant.

When the book finally begins to come together there is always the support of the editing and publishing team. Thanks also to Simon Fowler for his useful comments and suggestions in putting the chapters together and gathering suitable illustrations, and to John Thorpe who helped with information about the various textile processes and glossary, and to the many other people who provided countless stories, details and observations about the textile industry.

All illustrations are from the author's collection except:
extract from *Wool Record*, courtesy of World Textile Publications Ltd; OS maps courtesy of Ordnance Survey; School Leaving Certificate, Fred Riches, Factory Regulations Act certificate, Emma Riches and inventory of stock, courtesy of Mrs Glendinning; apprenticeship indenture, Knaresborough, courtesy of Teesside Archives; Cleator Strikers, courtesy of TUC Library Collection; Christine Shepherd at Geneva, courtesy of Christine Shepherd; trade-directory extracts, courtesy of The Historical Directories site from the University of Leicester at www.historicaldirectories.org; pirn winder, Paradise Mill, courtesy of Macclesfield Silk Museum; Dragon Hall, courtesy of The

Norfolk & Norwich Heritage Trust; frame-knitting machine, courtesy of Arkwright's Masson Mills, Matlock Bath, Derbyshire; ropewalk, Bewdley, courtesy of Bewdley Museum; long service and Defence of the Realm enquiries, courtesy of the Carpet Museum Trust, Kidderminster; Braintree Fountain and detail, courtesy of Roy Bracey; Gibson Mill, courtesy of Terry Teasdale.

As always, none of this would be possible without the support of my family and friends, who are, indeed, the fabric of my life.

INTRODUCTION

Since the day our cavemen ancestors discovered that life was more pleasant when wrapped up in a fur coat, textiles have been a part of our lives. Every country in the world has utilised its natural resources to provide fabric for clothes, to furnish houses, to wrap bodies in or to provide bags, baskets and belts, as well as countless other uses limited only by our imaginations and technical skills.

The first fabrics were constructed from either animal or plant materials, but nowadays there are many man-made fibres used either in conjunction with natural materials or on their own. Each has its own peculiarities and methods of production, though improvements in transport mean there is less emphasis on relying on local resources.

This section gives an overview of how the textile industry in England and Wales developed and moved from early times to modern times. The principal textiles looked at are wool, worsted, cotton, silk and linen, though the 'textile' industry has always consisted of a great variety of fabrics, used in a range of ways, and other branches are also considered.

House of Eumachia, Pompeii. This was the headquarters of the dyers.

The related industries expanded too. Textiles needed chemicals for a variety of treatments, finishes and dyes. By 1844 John Mercer had discovered a process that improved the properties of cotton, making it stronger, with a shiny finish that absorbed dye more easily. This became known as mercerised cotton. In 1856 William Perkin discovered a synthetic dye – aniline purple – and other synthetic dyes soon followed, though Germany rapidly became predominant in this field.

Machines were needed for the growing textile industry, giving rise to the symbiotic development of engineering in many of the textile towns.

Nowadays man-made fibres must be considered too, though they are only briefly examined here. The textile industry in the twentieth century has been on something of a roller coaster. There was a downturn at the beginning of the era, which was boosted hugely by the need for cloth during the First World War, with many firms making considerable profit. Britain was one of the first countries to industrialise but this meant that many of the machines were in use for decades. As other countries began their own industrialisation, they were able to start with better, faster, more efficient machines, many of them copied from British ones – or even bought in Britain and shipped abroad. British industry was slow to replace obsolete machinery and lost its competitive edge. With increasing globalisation, markets were lost to foreign trade and depression set in, being alleviated somewhat again by the intervention of war in 1939.

After the Second World War, textiles continued its long decline. For example, in 1950 the cotton mills in Lancashire employed 320,000 people, yet by 1982 they employed just 35,000. By 2005 this had fallen to about 7,200 (source: ONS – Annual Business Inquiry, 2005).

The increased use of synthetics, such as polyester, nylon and Terylene, required large injections of capital to fund specialised machinery rather than large numbers of skilled workers. The material could be produced anywhere in the world, no longer relying on natural raw materials. Businesses either folded or amalgamated, giving rise to large, dominant companies such as Courtaulds, Viyella International, English Sewing Cotton Company and Carrington & Dewhurst. Wages were held down and in the 1950s there was an increase in immigrant workers, from the Caribbean, from Poland during and after the war and from India and Pakistan from about 1960.

The older, family owned businesses began to die out as they were sold to larger multinational companies. In the 1970s there was a marked decline in the textile industry with a corresponding reduction in employment and value of cloth exported. Much cloth is now imported from abroad, particularly from Asia and China. The British textile industry has had to find niche markets of its own, producing small amounts of high-quality or specialised yarns. Design, clothing and fashion are becoming the most important aspects of the industry, with the East Midlands, the North West and London being the key areas for clothing, though textiles generally are still being produced in the traditional areas, including Yorkshire. In fact the designer fashion industry in Britain is one of the largest in the world, though it tends to be organised in smaller companies, rather than the conglomerates found elsewhere.

Today's textile industry is divided largely into four main sections:

• Suppliers that have a manufacturing base in Britain, which produce samples and small runs, but import larger orders from manufacturers abroad.
• Niche manufacturers that supply high-value but low-volume products.
• Limited manufacturing of high-quality yarn and technical clothing, especially fire-retardant textiles.
• Businesses that simply manage the design, production and distribution of merchandise that has been manufactured abroad.

Though no longer tied to any particular region, many textiles are still produced in the traditional areas – worsted and wool in West Yorkshire, cotton and technical textiles in the north west and knitted fabrics, clothing and carpets in the Midlands. The textile industry still employs about a 1/4 of a million people, whereas in 1901 the number was about 1 million.

The main focus of this book, however, is up to the mid-twentieth century before man-made fibres had made such a huge impact.

When tracing ancestors, knowing something about the industry in which they worked, how it developed, when and where it expanded and when and where it declined can be very helpful in tracking down when and where an ancestor might have moved. Some individual businesses are mentioned to illustrate different aspects of that branch of textiles, or how the industry affected a specific region. Records mentioned in the archives are exemplar rather than comprehensive – archives are collecting documents regularly so any investigation needs to begin with a search of The National Archives A2A (Access2Archives) website: www.nationalarchives.gov.uk/a2a.

Chapter 1

GETTING STARTED

The basic genealogical rule is to work from the 'known to the unknown'. Other principles include:

• Be systematic – make sure every person has their own record card or page and keep all related facts together.

• Keep focused – decide what you want to find out when visiting record offices and libraries and don't get sidetracked.

• Keep copies of all certificates and information found.

• Always keep reference details so that if you need to go back and check facts, you know exactly which document to look for – and you avoid looking at the same sources twice.

• Don't make leaps of faith – prove your research every step of the way, otherwise you could end up 'barking up the wrong tree'.

• Join a family history society – near where your ancestor lived and/or near where you live. They can provide invaluable help in finding or providing information and have experienced researchers who can give advice. No society dealing specifically with textile ancestors has been found, but most groups have knowledge of their own local industries.

1.1 In the beginning

Make detailed notes of everything you already know about the ancestor(s) who was involved with textiles. This is where you can write down 'Aunt Mabel said that . . .'. Later you will need to check the facts, but there is sometimes a grain of truth in family legends and for this reason they are worth recording at this point.

Draw up a draft family tree from these details, including approximate dates, names of towns lived in or possible work places.

1.2 Interviewing relatives

Try to arrange this sooner rather than later, but be aware that some elderly people may have reservations about 'digging up the past' – it probably means they know something they'd rather other people didn't know. Remember morals, attitudes and beliefs change over time – to find out that your great-grandmother was illegitimate may be no problem for you, but your grandmother may view the fact differently.

Take your draft family tree with you, along with any relevant photographs or memorabilia you have. These often spark further memories. Try to record or write down everything, even if there is no proof for the stories yet.

Once you have amassed these details, you need to undertake serious research.

1.3 Using archives and record offices

Staff are generally very helpful, but they do need to know what you are looking for. Many (but not all) are part of the CARN network (County Archives Research Network). On your first visit to a member archive you will need to obtain a CARN card by completing a form and producing suitable identification that includes your full name, address and signature, such as a driving licence or passport. The card can then be used at other archives.

Most archives require you to book an appointment in advance of your visit, and this gives you the opportunity of discussing which documents or microfilms you wish to see.

Always use pencil when examining archive documents and treat them with great respect.

1.4 Basic records

Arranging and recording baptisms, marriages and burials was generally the responsibility of the local parish, though records may not always be complete nor entirely accurate. Very few early registers survive but when, in 1598, it was ordered that the details should be recorded on parchment, which is more durable, some of the earlier entries were occasionally copied up. During the period of the Civil War and Commonwealth (1640–1660) records became even more haphazard and there are many gaps. Between 1653 and 1660 the Church no longer kept records as this became a civil duty.

Many of the early records are in Latin. After 1733 details were recorded in English, and marriages after 1754 required signatures of the couple and witnesses to be included. However, details are very short and rarely give occupations.

In 1812 a law, known as Rose's Act, required Anglican clergy to use specially printed registers with separate registers for baptisms, banns, marriages and burials. On baptisms the occupation and abode of the father is given; burials include age, abode and sometimes occupation of the deceased.

On 1 July 1837 a system of national registration was introduced into England and Wales, recording basic facts of birth, marriage and death. Microfilm copies of the indexes to the registers are frequently available in local libraries or record offices and these indexes are also now available online. The following websites are of great use:

• www.freebmd.org.uk/. This site includes a transcription of some of the Civil Registration index of births, marriages and deaths for England and Wales. The information is provided with no charge but is an ongoing project and so does not contain all records yet.

Commercial websites include:

• www.ancestry.co.uk/.

• www.bmdindex.co.uk/.

Certificates can be ordered online from the General Record Office at:

• www.gro.gov.uk/gro/content/certificates/.

You can also order certificates direct from the Register Office at which the event was registered, if the office is still in existence.

1.5 Census returns

Since 1801 there has been a census of the British population every ten years, with the exception of 1941. These censuses are closed for 100 years and, therefore, the next one to become available (at the time of writing) will be the 1911 census, which will be partially open in 2009. The earliest census records are primarily statistical and have no genealogical value. From 1841 family details were included, and more comprehensive information has been asked for at each subsequent census.

Censuses record who was living at a particular address. The 1841 census lists names, approximate ages, occupation and whether they were born in the county in which the census took place. After 1851 relationship to the head of the household is given as well as their actual place of birth, age and occupation. For those in business, details of the number of employees are usually given.

Many libraries or record offices have censuses for their local area on microfilm. The 1881 census can be viewed free of charge online at: www.familyhistoryonline.co.uk or at www.familysearch.org.

A useful website is www.familia.org.uk/about.html, which gives holdings for many libraries across the country.

There are many websites that have census details available on a pay-per-view basis, such as www.findmypast.com or www.ancestry.co.uk. The 1901 census is available at www.1901censusonline.com/. Other census details can also be accessed from this site.

1.6 Wills

In the past few working people made wills since they had very little in the way of personal possessions to leave. Those who progressed up the social scale and became mill owners needed to be more specific about the distribution of their assets after death.

Undercliffe Cemetery, Bradford.

The two most important courts in which wills were proved before 1858 were the Prerogative Court of Canterbury (PCC), which took precedence over all other courts, and the Prerogative Court of York (PCY). In general, anyone holding property in the north of England down to Nottinghamshire had their will proved in York, those in the south or Wales had their will proved in Canterbury, but it is not that simple. Where land was held in more than one county, wills were often proved in Canterbury even if the deceased lived in the north. PCC wills have been indexed and can be viewed at www.national archives .gov.uk/documentsonline. Those for PCY are housed at the Borthwick Institute (see p. 175) and are partially indexed on www.britishorigins .com.

All post-1858 wills for England and Wales can be viewed at the Probate Department of The Principal Registry Family Division, Probate Search Room, First Avenue House, 42–49 High Holborn, London, WC1V 6NP; tel: 020 7947 7000. If you cannot visit First Avenue House, you can write for a search and/or copy to The Postal Searches & Copies Department, York Probate Sub-Registry, Castle Chambers, Clifford Street, York, YO1 9RG, giving the full name, address and date of death of the deceased, stating what you require and enclosing the appropriate fee (currently £5). Indexes (or Calendars) to post-1858 wills for England and Wales can also be found in some probate registries around the country and in some record offices and archives. A guide to probate services can be found at www.hmcourts-service.gov.uk/cms/1226.htm.

The National Archives documents online has many records relating to wills of weavers, other textile workers and manufacturers, so it is worth searching under the various occupations.

1.6.1 Obituaries

Not surprisingly these are more likely to appear for mill owners and often they can be quite extensive. The larger the mill, the more influential the owner and therefore he warranted more space for his obituary. Sometimes libraries have a 'cuttings' section with these in or have a names index. Otherwise, look in newspapers around the date of death or burial. These entries often give a potted history of the person and/or the business itself.

APRIL 15, 1889   THE TEXTILE MANUFACTURER   165

Obituary.

Mr. John Bright.

AT the close of last month, all England, and indeed the whole English-speaking race, were called upon to mourn over the death of one of the most eminent of modern Englishmen. The name of John Bright was everywhere a household word, and friend and foe alike joined in paying the last tribute of respect to the memory of their distinguished countryman. His noble qualities of mind and heart, and his political and social labours have been recounted in every journal in the land, and nothing is required of us but to offer a brief account chiefly of his connection with the industry with which this Journal is more immediately concerned. Mr. Bright's family, according to the best authorities, came from Wiltshire, and in 1684 the ancestors of Mr. John Bright, on the paternal side, oldest in the family. Mrs. Bright was a woman of remarkable faculties, fond of poetry, clear-minded, and studious. She died on the 18th of June, 1830, when her son John was 18 years of age. Mr. Jacob Bright died on the 7th of July, 1851, at the age of seventy-six. Mr. Bright's father was, it appears, a man of considerable energy and business talent, and by the year 1823 he had so extended his business operations that he had no fewer than 7000 spindles at work. Soon the extent of his business compelled him to provide additional premises, and a new mill was built on Cronkeyshaw Common, where, in course of time, other mills were built. In 1836, however, a fire broke out in the larger of the new buildings, caused by the friction of a scutching machine, the whole building and machinery being destroyed, the damage amounting to £20,000. Although partly covered by the insurance, the fire was a serious loss to Mr. Bright. The mill was re-built in 1840, and thereafter the business prospered so much with the Brights that still larger mills were built. Other extensions have been made in more recent years, including the

MR. JOHN BRIGHT.

resided near the village of Lyneham, on a farm to which their own name was given. They were all members of the Society of Friends. The father of Mr. John Bright was the late Mr. Jacob Bright, who was born in the ancient city of Coventry, and whose father and mother, Jacob and Martha Bright, died when he was young. Mr. Bright's father served an apprenticeship with William Holme, who farmed land at New Mills, in Derbyshire, and also had a number of fustian looms. In the year 1802, two of his master's sons moved to Rochdale, where they built a cotton mill, Hanging Road Mill, and Mr. Bright's father settled there with them, marrying one of his master's daughters, and subsequently he prospered. He took the lease of a mill at Cronkeyshaw Common, Rochdale, in 1816, five years after the birth of his second son by his second wife, who was Miss Martha Wood, daughter of a tradesman of Bolton-le-Moors. They were married on the 31st of July, 1809, and had eleven children. The eldest, a boy, died at the age of four, and John, the future statesman, became the erection of a gigantic shed, and at the present time the firm of Bright Brothers carry on one of the most important establishments in the district, and employ no fewer than 1600 work-people. A remarkable impetus was given to the business by the introduction of Mr. Bright's sons into the concern as they respectively grew to manhood, and to their spirit, enterprise, and intelligent vigour the rapid extensions referred to were chiefly due. Mr. Jacob Bright, the father, retired from the firm in 1839, since which time the business has been continued under the style of "John Bright and Brothers." During the ten years that Mr. Bright represented Manchester the works were considerably extended, the business interests of his firm being looked after by Mr. Thomas Bright and Mr. Jacob Bright, while Mr. John Bright actively engaged himself in politics. In addition to the cotton spinning business commenced, and for so many years profitably carried on, by their father, Messrs. Bright Brothers entered largely into the carpet trade. In the course of this experiments and extension in this connection they found it necessary to adopt many improvements in machinery and appliances, and in doing

Obituary of John Bright, March 1889.

1.7 Cemeteries

As the Victorian era progressed, ever more elaborate monuments were erected to show off the accumulated wealth of a lifetime, such as those at Undercliffe Cemetery, Bradford. These may include details of many family members and give useful information. For the less fortunate, graves were often simply a grassy plot, but these may contain multiple burials. The details will be found in the cemetery records, which may include a grave book and burial register.

Records may be found in record offices or at the cemetery offices. Many local family history groups have transcribed monumental inscriptions (MIs) and published them with maps of the burial ground.

1.8 Charitable and benevolent institutions

Charity records may relate to orphanages, hospitals, almshouses and many other types of assistance. Children were frequently apprenticed from such charities and records may include apprenticeship indentures for children being supported by the charity. In Kirkham Parish, Lancashire, the Revd James Barker set up such a charity and it arranged many apprenticeships:

> Thomas Kirby with the consent of Edward Rawsthorn, Esq., Rev. Charles Buck, Rev. Robert Loxham, John Brance, John Langton, William Shepherd, Henry Lawson, John Loxtnand, John Birley, Trustees of the Charity of the Rev. James Barker, to John Lund of Kirkham, weaver, to be lodged by Jane Kirby during the term of his apprenticeship 18 Nov. 1755.

1.9 Friendly societies

You may find your ancestor belonged to an organisation such as the 'Buffaloes' or the 'Oddfellows'. Some grew from early local clubs, but in the early nineteenth century these often began when groups of men met in pubs, hence the prevalence of pubs with the names of friendly societies. The men may have simply helped each other out by each contributing a small amount and this grew into a specific subscription, from which members could draw in the event of hard times. Many related to a specific area or occupation and so remained small, for example the Friendly Society of Frame Work Knitters, founded in 1785, whose articles of association are in Nottinghamshire Archives.

Towards the end of the nineteenth century, the temperance movement grew and new friendly societies became linked with a 'non-alcoholic' approach, such as the International Order of Rechabites, founded in 1835, or the British Women's Temperance Association, founded in 1876.

Some also issued 'warrants' to members, which enabled them to find lodgings in other areas when looking for work. Quarter Sessions records often have settlement examinations (details taken from a 'stranger' to the district to establish where their legal settlement was, to which they would be returned if they needed to claim relief) that mention friendly societies. An example, from Lancashire Record Office:

> Notice of adjudication of settlement of the above Mary Speight, member of a Female Friendly Society 'at the house of William

Rippon the Bear and Staff in Lancaster' to be in West Derby' – ref QSP/2678/46 – date: 1815 14 Mar.

Many friendly societies keep their own records, though some are now depositing them with local record offices. The majority of these records comprise rules but others include more details. In 1855 the Friendly Society Act was passed and this required the societies to register, giving rise to lists of registered societies in specific areas and these may be found in local record offices.

1.10 Guilds and companies

The guilds or livery companies were responsible for checking the quality of produce and setting wages. Formed from the twelfth century onwards, one of the earliest was the Weavers' Guild, established in 1155. The guilds were social and charitable as well as occupational, so belonging to one provided many benefits. The guilds kept extensive records to ensure they knew who they had authorised to practise 'their' trade and many of these records survive, principally at the

The Guildhall, Carlisle.

Guildhall Library, City of London (see p. 159). Some of the guilds still exist, but their primary function nowadays is charitable. London guilds included Broderers (embroiderers), Clothworkers, Cordwainers (workers in fine leather), Curriers (dressers of tanned leather), Dyers, Girdlers (girdles and belts as clothing), Weavers and Woolmen (winders and packers of wool). Other areas also developed guilds, such as in the north east where the Society of Fullers and Dyers was founded in 1477, the Society of Weavers in 1527 and the Society of Rope Makers in 1648.

Originally, an apprentice became a freeman of the guild that represented his trade, but by the nineteenth century this link became more tenuous – he could have become a member of a different livery company or guild.

Guild influence was widespread, but had begun to decline by the end of the fifteenth century. Although many guild records have been lost, some survive and may include minutes of meetings with references to the men who attended, or in the case of the most influential guilds, details of the members themselves. Mention of guild members may also be found in wills, deeds, apprenticeship indentures and Quarter Sessions records.

Indexes to many London livery company records that are kept at the Guildhall Library have been published (Cliff Webb's *London Livery Company Apprenticeship Registers*). The indexes can be found in the library of the Society of Genealogists, at the Guildhall Library, and on their website, as well as on the British Origins website. These include the records of Dyers, Woolmen, Broderers, Feltmakers, Framework Knitters and Glovers. Other guild records are at the Guildhall Library, which also has printed guides to the records. Wills, or other legal documents, may include reference to an ancestor's livery company.

If an ancestor was a freeman of the City of London, records (from 1681 to 1923) are held at London Metropolitan Archives. There is also an index to city freedoms held in the Guildhall Library Manuscripts Section. Other record offices may have details of guilds formed in their area.

1.10.1 Merchant Taylors' Company

One of the earliest livery companies, it was founded in 1327, but by the seventeenth century had lost its link with the textile trade. The company records are found at the Guildhall Library and include details of charities and properties owned as well as membership and apprentice records. It was a very large company and had extensive records, some even dating back to the fourteenth century, although these are not complete. There is a comprehensive guide on their website (www.merchant-taylors.co.uk/) and in the Guildhall Library.

The following livery companies keep their own archives:

1.10.2 Clothworkers' Company

In 1528 the Fullers' Company and the Shearmen's Company joined together and formed the Clothworkers' Company. There are no extant records of the membership of either of the two original companies so the principal Registers of Freemen start in 1545. These have limited information – just the names and how they obtained their freedom, but later registers include more genealogical information. The Apprenticeship Registers, from 1606 but not indexed until 1718 and initially in Latin, include names of the apprentice and his father, their abode and the name of the master. Only those who worked in London are likely to be included in these registers and many of those working as clothier, weaver, tailor, draper, rug-maker or other similar occupation would have belonged to the Company. A complete list of Masters is to be found on the website (www.clothworkers.co.uk/) but there is no complete index of Wardens, Assistants or Liverymen until the twentieth century. Progression can be traced through the Court Orders, which are only partially indexed. Artisan clothworkers were unlikely to be promoted to the Livery and the archive includes very few records relating to members of the Yeomanry (the lower level of membership in former times).

Access requirements: general enquiries about the history of the Company and its archives will be answered by the Archivist without charge, but look at the information on the website first. The archive may be used by researchers from Monday to Friday, by appointment, at the discretion of the Company. Those wishing to consult the archive should apply in writing to the Archivist, giving details of their research and including a letter of introduction from a third party of suitable standing. The archive is a private resource and some items may not be available.

1.10.3 Drapers' Company

This organisation controlled the quality of woollen cloth traded in London, checking that only their members bought and sold cloth and that the quality and measurement were correct. Their archives include membership records from its earliest times, but also records of the charities they established. The archives are available for research by appointment. Contact the Drapers' Company, Drapers' Hall, Throgmorton Avenue, London EC2N 2DQ; tel: 0207 588 5001; email: mail@thedrapers.co.uk.

1.10.4 Mercers' Company

The records of the Mercers' Company date back to 1348. In its widest sense mercery could describe all merchandise, although in London the term evolved to mean the trade specifically in luxury fabrics, such as silk, linen, hemp-cloth and fustian, and in a large variety of miscellaneous 'piece goods', such as bedding, headwear, ribbons, laces and purses. Mercers' Company archives hold the historic records of the Mercers' Company from 1348 to the present, documenting every aspect of the history of the Company and its administration. The archives serve as the corporate memory for the Company, as well as providing a wealth of historical sources for academic research.

Record series of particular note include: Acts of Court (main minutes series of the Company), 1453 to the present; Company's account books from 1442; Company Charters and Ordinances; Registers of Members from 1348, and Registers of Apprentices, 1619 to 1888; and Minutes of the Joint Grand Gresham Committee from 1596 to the present. There is currently no access available to the archives by visiting researchers, but the Archivist will, wherever possible, help with any query and supply digital images of documents if required.

1.10.5 Merchant Adventurers

By the end of the sixteenth century the Merchant Adventurers were funding exploration with a view to trade. Four major companies were set up at this time:

The Russia or Muscovy Company (1555)

Established factories, such as Thornton's Woollen Mill, in St Petersburg. Around Cronstadt and St Petersburg there was a surprisingly large English sector and over the years many English textile firms traded with Russia. The company provided a church for the settlement, together with a minister who recorded births, marriages and deaths. Though many original records were lost in 1666, surviving records, or copies, for both company and church, can be found in the Guildhall Library.

The Levant or Turkey Company (1581)

Traded mainly with Turkey and the Middle East, exporting, among many other items, cloth and importing raw silk, cotton, indigo dye, wool and cotton cloth. Records for this company are at The National Archives. Some are in the Secretaries of State: State Papers Foreign, but also in the Board of Trade: Companies Registration Office: Files of Dissolved Companies. Some petitions by or against the Levant Company may be found in the Privy Council papers. A 'Quick Search' using 'Levant Company' from the home page of The National Archives website will find these documents. The same search on the A2A search page will produce a list of documents at various repositories relating mainly to correspondence between the Levant Company and other businesses.

The East India Company (1600)

The India Office Records include the archives of the East India Company (1600–1858) and are to be found in The British Library. Trading included extensive imports and involvement in the cotton and calico trade. There is an online searchable database, which does not just contain information relating to those who had a direct connection with textiles. A search using the word 'cotton' brought up, among many others, details of Frank Applegath, born 28 February 1822, Lambeth, Surrey, son of Augustus, a cotton and silk printer, but also the marriage of Mary Haydock, in 1920, Madras, to Frank Smethurst, cotton-mill foreman.

The Hudson Bay Company (1670)

This is the only one still in existence. It was significant for imports of beaver fur, which was extensively used in the hat trade, especially in London, but its records are unlikely to have any relevance to ancestors who worked in the textile trade as such. Records are kept in the provincial archives in Manitoba, Canada, with microfilm copies in

The National Archives. There is a searchable database on their website: www.gov.mb.ca/chc/archives/hbca/about/hbca.html. This is currently being expanded to cover HBC employees.

1.11 Government sources

The House of Lords and, particularly the House of Commons Select Committees, have held inquiries into most aspects of British life. They include investigations into the state of trade, such as the Select Committee report on the silk trade of March 1832. Many committees interviewed both workers and employers. Records of these proceedings are housed at The Parliamentary Archives. The easiest way to search is by using the Chadwyck-Healey Index to the House of Commons Parliamentary Papers, which is a digitised set of Parliamentary Papers, available in the reading rooms in The National Archives Library on the computer terminals. University libraries and large central libraries may also have copies of the original books and indexes. For example, Bradford Library holds a printed volume of the Report of the Commissioners on the Employment of Children in Factories (1833). The Commissioners travelled the country interviewing manufacturers, mill owners and factory workers to find out about their conditions of work. As a result of this investigation the 1834 Factory Act was passed, restricting the working hours of children. There are full descriptions of each mill included and a brief history given where known. Even if your ancestor is not mentioned, the report makes fascinating reading.

Name	Age	Trade	Disorder	Weeks sick	Sum received	Remarks
Ashcroft, Esther	27	Hand loom Weaver	Debility	1	£0 4s 0d	
Beswick, Elizabeth	26	Power loom weaver	Consumption	17	£1 4s 0d	Dead £2 7s 0d allowed for coffin
Tong, Ann	14	Reeler	Cholera	4	£0 16s 0d	

Entries from the Bolton Parish Church Sunday School Sick Society register, 1883.

There are lists of questions put and the answers given – many are fairly general, relating to hours of work and payments made. Individual interviews with workers give much more personal detail but it is a matter of pot luck whether your ancestor appears or not.

In some cases there are reports on sickness benefits, such as those from the Bolton Parish Church Sunday School Sick Society (established 2 June 1816). About 580 members subscribed a penny per week and received an allowance of 2s to 4s per week during sickness or until the amount reached £7 6s (£7.30). If the person was an orphan, relief continued at the discretion of officers. An allowance of about £2 was paid for funeral expenses.

1.11.1 Taxation

The office of ulnager (aulnager) was instituted in 1312 to regulate the length, width, weight and general quality of cloth. Another aspect of the ulnager's job was, of course, to ensure that the correct tax was paid. This office only ended officially in 1724, though it was never particularly effective. Ulnage records, where they exist, are at The National Archives holdings of the records of King's Remembrancer Accounts in series E101. Oxford ulnage dates from 1377 and named ulnagers include Richard More and William Hyde (1467/8). Ulnage receipts are lists of clothiers with sums paid and numbers of cloths sealed, examples include Godalming, Farnham, Petworth and Midhurst for 1574–1587 with a further set of receipts for Godalming for 1585. The More Molyneux family, whose records are also in the Surrey History Centre, held the office of Ulnager for Surrey and Sussex for much of the first half of the sixteenth century and their family records also refer to this. Ulnage accounts for Southampton, Winchester and Hampshire generally are at The National Archives E101 series, including some names of clothiers, but some ulnage accounts remain both in the Chamberlains' account rolls of the fifteenth century in Hampshire Archives. A useful guide to medieval customs accounts can be found in The National Archives Guides.

Pipe Rolls, many of which have been transcribed by the Pipe Roll Society, record taxation from 1155 onwards. Some of these may refer to merchants and clothiers. A guide to the use of Pipe Rolls can be found in The National Archives.

In 1353 Edward III imposed a duty on each sack of wool, known as the Ordinance of the Staple. All wool had to be exported through the 'staple towns' (initially Bristol, Canterbury, Carmarthen, Chichester, Exeter, Lincoln, Newcastle-upon-Tyne, Norwich, Westminster, Winchester and York) to Calais, to ensure that the Company of the Staple of Calais collected the correct duty. Since this monopoly effectively pushed up the price of wool exports, it gradually became more profitable to make the cloth in England, rather than buying it in from Europe. It also became more lucrative to smuggle wool out of England and this 'trade' also increased.

From a situation where Government had very little to say about how a business should be run, the Industrial Revolution and its aftermath forced Parliament to bring in new laws that now cover almost every aspect of our working life. These laws and the inquiries that often preceded them are well documented in Parliamentary Papers and provide a wealth of information about how our ancestors viewed their employment. The documents are available at The National Archives, which holds a complete set on microfilm.

1.12 Family and estate records

Records for buildings may be kept with the estate papers in private ownership; others have been deposited with local record offices. They may be found with estate agent or solicitors' records or under the name of the landowner. It is therefore necessary to track down the local landholders, some of whom may be charities or local institutions rather than an individual or family. The actual landowner may live in a totally different area and thus the records will be a considerable distance away. For example, Cumbria Record Office holds records relating to the Howard Family of Corby Castle, Cumberland, including a deed dated 1800 of a seventeen-year lease by Henry Howard of his fulling mill (also referred to as a Walkmill) on Cairn brook, which eventually became known as Glencairn Mill. The same group of records includes a deed dated 1303 relating to a twenty-year lease by Lord John de Greystok to William, son of Lambert de Dernton and Galfrid de Langgeton, fullers of the High Coniscliffe, County Durham.

Many mills changed their use over the years and so may be more difficult to track down. Some were demolished, converted to dwellings (as is presently very often the case) or used for a different industry altogether. Where records are kept in private hands, it is not always possible to see them. Where access is available, a charge may sometimes be made.

1.13 Education

As Britain became a more industrialised society it became obvious that the workforce required educating. This comprised both basic 'Three Rs' education and more technical training.

1.13.1 Schools

Sunday schools were often linked to churches or Non-conformist chapels, some of which date back to the sixteenth century. Records are likely to be found with other parish records. The majority of school records that are useful to family historians date from the nineteenth century. Most have now been deposited in record offices.

Many factory owners were frequently involved in local schools, both in terms of providing some funding and in the general running of the institution. Records are likely to be similar to those kept by other charities, such as minute books and subscription lists. Some mill owners provided land to enable schools to be built or money to set up libraries.

Other records include:

• Log books – dating from about 1840, these provide general information on the school and comments on pupils. Some may include governors' minute books.

• Admission registers – kept after the 1870 Education Act and include the name of the child, date of birth, date of admission to the school, father's name, address and sometimes occupation, name of any previous school and the date of leaving.

1.13.2 Mechanics' Institutes

Mechanics' Institutes were started in order to provide scientific and technical training for the workers who had limited education or opportunities, and usually included subjects relevant to local industry. Employers not only subscribed to these organisations, and so appeared in the financial records of the institute, but also sat on the board of management.

Many institutes eventually joined with other local organisations to become technical colleges, which in turn often evolved into polytechnics and later universities. The records may therefore be in local record offices or in local university archives.

Mechanics' Institute, Huddersfield.

Records may include:

• Class rolls – giving occupation, employer, address, previous education, present attainments and position in classes.

• General registers – which also included occupation, age, entry date, residence, but also may give details of the students' successes in each subject such as cloth manufacture, wool dyeing, weaving and pattern designing.

• Finance reports and annual reports – may give primarily financial or just general information but may also detail specific students or winners of scholarships etc.

• Committee minutes – may make specific mention of individual students, appointment and resignation of teachers as well as committee members. Sub-committees for specific aspects of the running of the institute, such as buildings, will have separate minute books.

- Subscription lists – these may refer to the 'subs' paid by members for the classes attended, in which case names, addresses and employers will generally be included, or may also refer to subscriptions paid towards specific needs, such as new buildings or for major maintenance. In this case, they may be included with special committee records and generally list names of subscribers, who may be individuals or companies, together with the amount of their donation.

- Membership records.

- Deeds, leases and papers relating to trustees of the institute.

- Photographs.

- Fire-insurance policies.

- Examination papers and results.

Exam results were often reported in local newspapers.

1.14 Newspapers, magazines and journals

Though newspapers or journals, as they were usually called, began to be printed during the seventeenth century, they contained very little local news. They concentrated on events in London, politics and the Court, since that was the focus of the literate few. As education became more widespread, they began to include local events and views until they developed into the form we have now – national and local newspapers.

The print used in newspapers tends to be small and the pages are crammed with detail. Contents include advertisements for local business products, job vacancies, reports of local court cases and events. Local elections, in which mill owners often took part, are reported at length. Later, letters from readers are included and births, deaths and marriages sections appear. There is rarely any index but some record offices or libraries may have limited indexes to subjects or names. Sales of business premises, often giving names of occupiers, can be found.

Some of the more useful sources are:

- *London Gazette* – published from 1665, when it was originally called the *Oxford Gazette*, it provided up-to-date information on events of national importance. Interesting to read for its historical value, although it concentrated on London news, it also contained details of all bankruptcies. These are now fully searchable online at: www.gazettes-online.co.uk/.

• *Gentleman's Magazine* – published from 1731 to 1907, it gave summary details of some news events, including births, deaths and marriages for upper and some middle-class families, as well as bankruptcies. Each volume is indexed and there are surname indexes from 1731–1810 and obituary indexes from 1731–1819. The indexes up to 1855 can be found in the Guildhall Library and the newspapers can be searched online at: www.bodley.ox.ac.uk/ilej/journals/srchgm.htm.

• Times Digital Archive – a database of all issues of *The Times* newspaper from 1785 to 1985, often available via your local library.

• Both *The Times* and the *Guardian* now have online archives, available via their main websites: www.timesonline.co.uk/tol/news/ and www.guardian.co.uk.

In addition, a large number of nineteenth-century newspapers have been digitised and are available online at university libraries, The National Archives and the British Library itself www.bl.uk/collections /newspapers.html (see also p. 142)). University libraries often have microfilm copies of a variety of newspapers and magazines. Copies of a wide range of newspapers and journals are held at the British Library (Newspapers).

Most local libraries hold copies of newspapers for their own area. In these will be found reports of mill trips, parties held to celebrate Christmas, special events in the life of the mill or the mill owners, such as weddings and the coming-of-age of the family sons. These reports will sometimes refer to individuals, though these are usually mill managers or supervisors. Workers rarely get full obituaries unless they did something notable such as falling into a dye vat and getting killed, when there will also be details of coroners' inquests. Sometimes other events became newsworthy, for example, the story of Sam Wilson. In 1930 Sam Wilson retired and was presented with an armchair by the directors of Messrs J Robson & Sons at Dalton Dye Works. This in itself might have resulted in a small paragraph but Sam had two brothers, George and Charlie, all sons of John Wilson of Huddersfield. All three sons were employed by the same firm, working there all their lives: Sam for fifty-seven years, Charlie fifty-two and George fifty years. George took active part in the trade union, friendly society and Co-operative Movement and was then the oldest member of the Dyers Union; both George and Charlie were members of Cornwallis Lodge of Oddfellows; George served for many years on the Board and Education Committee of Huddersfield Industrial Society.

Some libraries have newspaper-cuttings books or name indexes for such items in their local newspaper.

1.14.1 Trade journals

Many of the individual trades had their own newspapers or trade journals, such as the *Wool Record*, published in Bradford from the beginning of the twentieth century and still in production, and the *Cotton Factory Times*, published in Manchester from 1885 until 1937. The British Library holds a complete set of trade journals and most libraries and record offices hold some copies of newspapers relevant to

Extract from the Wool Record, *1 January 1914.*

their local area. For example, in their Business Record section, Greater Manchester County Record Office holds copies of: *Textile Weekly*, 1928–1967, *Textile Manufacturer*, 1897–1914, *Textile Recorder*, 1884–1967, *Man Made Textiles*, 1956–1967, *Silk and Rayon*, 1934–1954, *British Rayon and Silk Journal*, 1949–1954, *Silk Journal*, 1924–1934, *Rayon Record*, 1929–1933 and *Silk Journal and Rayon World*, 1934–1949.

The *Textile Manufacturer*, published in Manchester between 1875 and 1978, is described as 'A practical journal for mill owners, machinists, dyers, calico printers, bleachers etc'. A column entitled 'Jottings and Useful Hints' included almost anything related to the trade, often events or accidents at various mills, but there is also a range of articles about the industry both at home and abroad, occasional reports on individual companies, trade reviews for different areas, lists of dividends declared by limited companies, bankruptcies and dissolutions of partnerships of firms connected with textiles, together with lists of new companies formed, names of their shareholders and where they lived. The shareholders are not, as one might expect, just 'old moneyed' families. By the late nineteenth century, some skilled workers were also joining together to form companies:

Robert Hartley and Co Ltd, registered 21st ult [December 1888] capital of £3000 in twenty pound shares to trade as spinners and manufacturers of cotton, woollen or other fibrous substance:

Subscribers			Shares held
Robert Hartley	Burnley	bookkeeper	10
W Rushton	Burnley	loom tackler	10
R Riley	Burnley	loom tackler	10
R Whalley	Burnley	beamer	10
E Wilkinson	Burnley	loom oiler	10
R H Horsfall	Burnley	cloth looker	10
J Howarth	Burnley	cloth looker	10
J T Sharples	Burnley	weaver	10
T Berry	Burnley	drawer-in	10

Articles and explanations of new laws, their impact on the textile industry and relevant court cases are included:

A case of considerable importance was heard last month at the Mansfield Police Court in which Messrs H J and E H Greenhalgh spinners and doublers of Mansfield were summoned at the instance of the Extra Hard Cotton Twist Spinners Association for infringement of the Merchandise Marks Act of 1887 in having reeled and sent out yarn of less than 840 yards to the hank and in having labelled the yarn as 60's twist. They were fined £2 in each of the two cases in addition to the payment of costs which amounted to £120.

Perhaps the most important information is given in the large number of obituaries. These range from full-page spreads with pictures for important people to brief outlines for the less well known. But most give some history of the person and often of any businesses too. The obituary for Frederick W Hill of Bradford, on 20 June 1888, mentions his age (56 years), that he started work with Messrs Craven and Harrop of Bradford, went into partnership with Nathan Drake as Messrs Hill and Drake, before starting his own business as F W Hill & Co. in a factory at New Leeds. Hill was also a member of Bradford Corporation for many years and served on the Board of Management at Bradford Infirmary. The obituary of Richard McDiarmid, who was connected with cotton spinners in Bollington and Macclesfield, states that he 'has acted on several occasions as deputy from the Spinnners' Association in disputes'. He was also president of the Ashton-under-Lyne Branch of the Cotton Spinners' Society for twenty-five years.

Company magazines

Most companies have 'house' magazines that give details of happenings in the company, company clubs and societies and special occasions. Businesses often had their own football or cricket clubs and played in the local textile league. Retirements, promotions, marriages or obituaries also featured. Though each magazine may be indexed, it is rare to find any comprehensive index to a series of magazines, so the approximate date of the event will be needed before searching for further information.

Union magazines and journals

Some of these are specific to 'labour' interests but may not have always kept the same name. For example, the *Yorkshire Factory Times* started in July 1889 and ended in September 1910. When it started up again, it changed its name to the *Labour Pioneer* and remained as this from November 1919 to June 1922, when it changed its name yet again to the *Yorkshire Factory Times and Workers Weekly Record*, which it retained until it ceased publication in April 1926.

Across the Pennines the non-partisan *Cotton Factory Times* was published weekly from 1885 until 1937. Magazines not only documented current concerns but often gave details of 'special' events – someone with a long work history or achieving promotion. You may also find obituaries for anyone who took an active part in unionism.

1.15 Oral and photographic archives

Many libraries have oral histories, indexed by name, date and/or topic. Photographic collections may include factory buildings and workers, though workers names are rarely known. Some photographic archives are now available online:

• Tameside Image Archive – currently includes over 20,000 images and is being added to regularly. The images can be viewed and purchased online at: www.tameside.gov.uk/history/archive.php3.

• English Heritage Photo Library – includes images of historic buildings from all over England. 'Viewfinder' is a library of general images, which may include workers, and 'Images of England' has images of listed buildings. Access online at: www.english-heritage.org.uk/server/show/nav.1506.

A selection of mill histories.

• Leodis – a photographic collection created by Leeds Library and Information Service of Leeds from the nineteenth century to date. Its 50,000-image collection includes many images of mills and workers. Access online at: www.leodis.net/.

• BBC Family History – Your Photos collection contains images submitted by individuals covering a wide range of topics. It is searchable by keyword, theme, date or region. You can also scan and send your own photographs to add to the database. Access online at: www.bbc.co.uk/history/familyhistory/your_photos/.

• Staffordshire Past Track – a project to digitise material from the area and includes, among others, many images of textile mills and shoe factories. Access online at: www.staffspasttrack.org.uk/.

1.16 Maps

Ordnance Survey maps developed from the 1740s when they were needed for military purposes. Maps from 1819 are usually 1in-to-the-mile scale, but by the 1860s maps of 6in and even 25in were available. These maps can be useful in locating a specific mill or working out

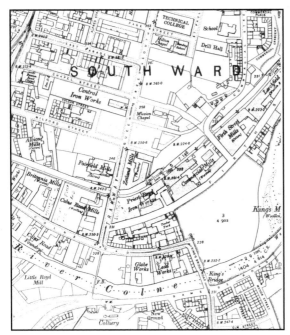

An Ordnance Survey map of Huddersfield, with mills, 1893.

when it might have been built or demolished. Different series of maps show varying detail. Historical Ordnance Survey maps can be found online at: www.old-maps.co.uk/. The British Library also has some useful information about the different series available: www.bl.uk/collections/map_os.html.

Maps were also produced for different purposes. The earliest maps were private maps of estates for the landowner. Tithe maps date from 1836. Tithes were the amount of goods claimed by the Church as 'God's Tithe'. The right to the tithes passed to individuals when the monasteries were closed in the sixteenth century and by the nineteenth century many people objected to paying them. The Tithe Act allowed the tithes to be commuted to a monetary payment or to be compensated by land allocation when the common land was enclosed. Tithe maps and apportionments are very detailed and show who owned each field, who occupied it and the purpose of land and buildings. Many areas are now putting tithe maps online, such as Cheshire at: maps.cheshire.gov.uk/tithemaps, and Wales at the National Library of Wales: www.llgc.org.uk/.

Fire-insurance maps relate to building use (see p. 57).

1.17 Mill histories

Firms frequently produced booklets for special events, such as visit by royalty or to commemorate an anniversary of the mill building or business. These publications often contain pictures of processes, departments or workers, though not always with names. Many will be found in local libraries but some were also given to employees as commemorative gifts. There has been a big increase in interest in our industrial and local heritage so more of these are now available.

1.18 Personal records

These may include letters, diaries and other personal notes. Some will be with family papers but others may have ended up with business papers and will therefore be found in business records. For example, when members of the Wilde family moved to St Petersburg, Russia, in the 1880s to run the Thornton Woollen Mill there, they wrote letters back to the family in Huddersfield, describing weather and events in Russia.

As part of their training, sons were often sent abroad to oversee or learn more about the trade by working in overseas branches (Australia,

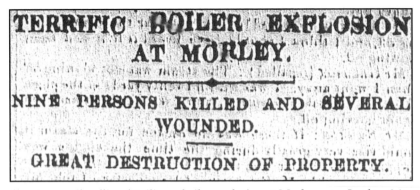

A newspaper headline detailing a boiler explosion at Morley, near Leeds, 1863.

Argentina, Canada, America and India), and many wrote letters home that have survived.

Some workers, too, wrote personal histories of their working life that may have been published or simply printed in pamphlet form. Some may be available in libraries or record offices. Diaries may give very specific details of events and conditions in local mills, but are very rare.

1.19 Accidents in the workplace

Mills were dangerous places to work in. There were numerous cases of workers having limbs ripped off by the machinery, falling into the dye vats or losing an eye when a shuttle flew out. The buildings were major fire hazards – the massive mill chimneys often collapsed and the boilers seem to have exploded regularly. All these accidents were recorded and, in the case of a death, details from the inquest were often included almost verbatim, giving information not only about the victim(s) but the witnesses too. Full details of these events were usually reported in the newspapers.

1.19.1 1897 Workmen's Compensation Act record book

This law established the 'no fault' principle, which allowed the injured workers to claim compensation without having to prove that their injury or illness had been the result of employer negligence. Records were kept giving the date of the accident, name of injured personnel, age, department/occupation, average wage earned, injury, number of weeks off work and compensation paid. On 30 July 1898 Lizzie

Marsden, 21, a filler in the print shed at Crossley's carpet factory, Halifax, suffered a torn hand. Her average wage was 12s, and she was away from work for eight weeks. She received £1 14s 9d (£1.74) compensation. Deaths were also noted. These can then be followed up through coroners' reports and newspaper articles.

It was not only accidents and deaths that were reported. After the 1833 Factory Act, which made it illegal for children under 9 to work in factories, inspectors were appointed to enforce the Act. Their prosecutions were reported in the newspapers and some of their reports may be found in local record offices. Businesses had to keep 'Factory Inspector's Registers' to show that they were abiding by the law. For example, Wilton & Swindon Archives have the registers for Samuel Salter and Co., Trowbridge, Wiltshire, woollen manufacturers, which include certificates of provision of fire escape and a register of young persons under 18, which includes name, address and date of first employment. There are also certificates of fitness for employment for those under 16, with parents' names, date of birth, details of accidents and cases of poisoning or disease recorded.

Early health and safety records can be found at The National Archives in the Ministry of Labour records. A useful guide can be found at: www.nationalarchives.gov.uk/catalogue/rdleaflet.asp?sLeafletID=254.

1.20 Aliens and immigrants

Many immigrants began work in the textile industry. Once established here, searching for them follows the same pattern as for any other individual, but tracing them to their country of origin may not be as easy.

A useful website is www.movinghere.org.uk/, which gives full details of how to trace ancestry from abroad. Many local record offices and libraries also now have specific sections relating to immigrants who have settled in that area.

The National Archives records include HO 213 Aliens Office. Until 1905 immigrants had to register on arrival and a certificate was sent to the Aliens Office. This department also holds some files relating to internment camps, 1914–1948.

Correspondence regarding treatment of aliens is in HO213/494-8. Other information is in HO45 and (PRO) HO144 under subject headings 'Aliens', 'Nationality' and 'War'. HO215 Internment: General Files, 1940–1951, includes nominal camp lists arranged by name of camp, so are useful provided you know where your ancestor was held.

BT26 – Ships' Passenger Manifests has inward passenger lists from 1878–1888 and 1890–1960 but not from the Mediterranean or Europe.

Some groups did receive Government support on arrival. See: T93 – French; PMG53 – Spanish; MH8 – Belgians; HO294 – Czechs; and WO315 – Poles.

During both world wars, some foreigners were interned. Few records survive from the First World War but there are more extensive records for the Second World War:

HO45 and HO144 – First World War records. HO39 – microfilm copies of individual name cards. See also HO214.

1.20.1 Naturalisation

Not everyone bothered to become naturalised, and before 1844 it required an Act of Parliament. There are some records of denization (which gave some rights but not full naturalised rights) and naturalisation from the fifteenth century at The National Archives, but these were also published in the *London Gazette*, which is now available online at: www.gazettes-online.co.uk.

Records at The National Archives that may contain useful information include: HO405 – applications for naturalisation between

The Jewish Museum, Manchester.

1934 and 1948; HO2 – certificates of aliens arriving in Britain between 1836 and 1852, arranged by port of arrival. These are unindexed, apart from an index to German arrivals that is in the Research Enquiries Room at The National Archives; HO3 – lists of immigrants arriving from Europe between 1836 and 1869, completed by the ship's master.

1.20.2 Huguenot ancestry

The best place to begin is with the Huguenot Society, which has done a great deal of transcription of original documents and has extensive knowledge of Huguenots in Britain. Contact the Society at: The Huguenot Library, The Huguenot Society, University College London, Gower Street, London, WC1E 6BT; website: www.huguenot society.org.uk/.

At The National Archives the Exchequer Subsidy Rolls (E179) include rolls of names of foreigners living around London, 1523–1561. Exchequer Accounts Various (E101) includes details of transactions in which foreign merchants resident in London were concerned. Parliament Rolls often contain a record of Acts of Naturalisation from about 1400. Patent Rolls (C66 and C67) record the grants of Denizations by Letters Patent from about 1400 to 1844, and Close Rolls (C54) have enrolments of Naturalisation Certificates granted between 1844 and 1873. State Papers often include references to 'strangers' around London, often with names of Huguenots from France and Walloons from the Netherlands.

In the Treasury Board Papers and In-letter (T1) there are many references to refugees who received payments. Names are indexed in the Calendar of Treasury Papers (1557–1728). There are also Embarkation Lists from The Hague in a bundle of In-letters (T1/119) of Palatine subjects transported from Holland to England in 1709.

1.20.3 Jewish ancestry

The National Archives records in HO2 include certificates of arrival for many Jews arriving in England between 1836 and 1852. These are partly indexed in HO5. HO3 includes masters of ships' returns for 1836 to 1869. These are mostly unindexed, but the Metzner index at The National Archives lists Germans, Pole and Prussians arriving between 1847 and 1852, including many Jews.

Other useful sources include:

• Jewish Museum, 190 Cheetham Hill, Manchester, M8 8LW; tel: 0161

834 9879; email: info@manchesterjewishmuseum.com; website: www.manchesterjewishmuseum.com. The museum also holds some records relating to the Jewish community in the area.

• The Jewish Museum, 4 Shakespeare Road, London, N3 1XE; tel: 0208 371 7373; email: admin@jewishmuseum.org.uk; website: www.jewish museum.org.uk. The museum also holds some records relating to the Jewish community in the area.

• Greater Manchester Police Museum, 57a Newton Street, Manchester, M1 1ES; tel: 0161 856 3287; email: police.museum@gmp.police.uk; website: www.gmp.police.uk/mainsite/pages/history.htm. The museum also holds a Register of Aliens that includes many Jews.

1.20.4 The Commonwealth

The 1962 Immigration Act introduced an employment-voucher scheme for migrants from the Commonwealth. These were issued under one of three categories:

• Category A – for applications by employers in this country who have a specific job to offer to a particular Commonwealth citizen.

• Category B – for applications by Commonwealth citizens without a specific job to come to but with certain special qualifications, such as doctors or teachers.

• Category C – for all others.

These vouchers often contain a wealth of detail, including correspondence, occupation and dates of birth and photographs.

Some work permits for aliens to 1972 and, from 1973 onwards, from both aliens and Commonwealth citizens, are in The National Archives record series (PRO) LAB48 and LAB42.

HO334 includes duplicates of the certificates of British nationality declared by a British subject of a colony, protectorate or protected state. Unfortunately these are arranged by certificate number rather than by name. The names indexes to the certificates are at the Home Office Immigration and Nationality Department, Liverpool Nationality Office, B4 division, India Buildings, Water Street, Liverpool L2 0QN. Restrictions apply to those issued less than thirty years ago.

The National Archives record HO334/1988-2445, covering the period 1973–1981, is for certificate numbers 300001–414400, which appear to be principally Pakistanis.

HO334/2446-3436, covering period 1973–1982, and 500001-857706, are for other colonies/Commonwealth countries with a few Pakistanis, foreign women married to British subjects and minors. These files are still inaccessible under the thirty-year closure period.

There has been a black community in Britain since the sixteenth century but this increased considerably after the Second World War, when many were recruited due to a labour shortage here. Records may be found in passenger lists and naturalisation archives, but until 1962 Britain's colonial subjects were also British subjects and did not need to naturalise. After this date, they had to register as British citizens.

Electoral registers for the area in which an ancestor lived may include details, and these can be found at local record offices or libraries.

Ethnic communities or associations published their own newspapers as well as newsletters, annual reports of the mosques, temples, gurdwaras and churches for their communities, and these may give relevant information. Some of them may be found in local libraries or record offices.

Many local studies libraries and archives are now bringing together collections relating to minority communities in their areas. These may include documents, correspondence and oral histories.

Chapter 2

SOURCES FOR WORKERS

These fall into a number of different categories, including business records, such as staff/wages books, records created because of legislation, such as medical certificates, war records, union records and personal records, such as apprentice papers.

2.1 School Leaving Certificate

The passing of the 1870 Education Act and various Factory Acts made the employment of children under 10 illegal. The school leaving age was set between 10 and 14, but the child had to have a certificate showing that they had attained a minimum level of education before they could leave school. These may be with family documents but many employers kept them for inspection if required, and some have survived.

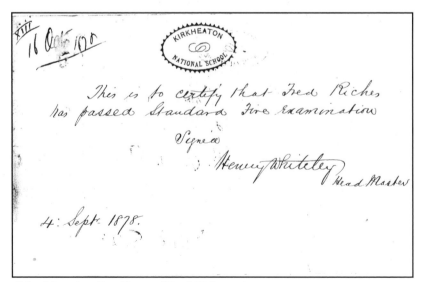

School Leaving Certificate of Fred Riches, 1870s.

2.2 Factory Regulations Act

The Factory Regulations Act of 1844 regulated the employment of women and young persons between the ages of 13 and 18. Employers therefore had to ensure that children were employed legally and had a certificate from a doctor confirming their age. All the doctor could actually do was to look at the child and confirm that 'the said Young Person has the ordinary strength and Appearance of a Young Person of at least Thirteen Years of Age and that I believe the real Age of the said Young Person to be at least Thirteen Years'. The doctor would generally rely on the parents to confirm the child's age but the certificate does provide a rough guide to age as well as giving the child's name, parents' names, address (at least the general area or village) and a date, together with the signature of the doctor.

These certificates were kept in a book that was printed with the name and address of the business. Some have survived as complete books and it is possible to find whole families having their children certified as fit to work in the mill.

2.3 Wages book

Some give full details, such as name, address, department in which employee worked and amount paid, but they are not always so

Factory Regulations Act certificate of Emma Riches, 1870s.

helpful. It is certainly possible to follow earnings and days worked or who worked in the different departments but often little else, as names are not always given in full. Sometimes just a surname is used, or initial and surname.

When a name disappears from the wage book it could be because the person has died, has moved to a different department that is not shown in the wage book or has moved to another employer. For women workers, she may have simply changed her name on marriage or have left to have a baby. She may then return to work some time later and appear again in the wages book under her married name.

2.4 Personnel records

These they can be invaluable, but have access restrictions, sometimes of about thirty years. In addition, sometimes firms may place further restrictions on all or parts of the documents deposited.

Under the 1911 National Insurance Act, all wage-earners aged between 16 and 70 earning less than £160 per year (raised to £250 in 1919, and to £420 in 1942) were obliged to contribute 4d per week, while employers paid 3d and the government 2d. Records had to be kept to show the employee/employer contributions and these may survive in personnel records. As these were generally completed by the employee themselves there is the chance of seeing an ancestor's handwriting too. The cards will also show name, address, occupation, department working in, date of starting, pay number, age last birthday and date of last birthday. Later, marital status was added.

These documents, where they have survived, are not generally indexed but just stored by first-letter order. Sometimes further comments may be written on the forms. When Benjamin Bowman, a single lad from Hipperholme, began work as a stoker at Crossley's carpet factory in Halifax he also gave his last occupation as 'coaling at Austin's, Birmingham'. He worked in the engineering department at Crossley's, but, since he was only 23 and the form was dated 1917, he should have been in the Army. A scribbled note at the bottom of the form explained that he had an Army discharge card dated 24 March 1917 for shell-shock.

Sometimes there are certificates for numerous members of the same family, since working in mills was frequently an occupation that engaged the whole family, but it is also possible to trace the movements of an individual. In November 1913 Mary Boland, of Dover Street,

Halifax, age 15, started work at Crossley's mill as a filler in the print shed. She had become a reeler in E mill five years later, while her younger brother, Andrew, began in June 1917 as a bobbin setter in Room 3, E mill. In December he transferred to Room 4 as a doffer, then moved again in October the following year to 7D mill as an assistant steamer. Their brothers John and Joseph also worked at the same mill.

2.4.1 Young persons' register

These should have been kept for all employees under the age of 18 when first employed. They include: surname, first name, address, date of first employment, date of leaving employment, date of birth, 'condition' (i.e., whether single or married), signature of doctor granting certificate to work, or certificate refused, and the date examined.

These are in date order not alphabetical and no reason is given for any refusal of certificate to work. Conditions imposed are generally simply 'to wear glasses', 'to pass eye examination' or 'to be seen at next visit'. The date of birth had to be confirmed from the birth certificate, so this can be taken as accurate.

2.4.2 Miscellaneous lists

Lists of specified personnel were compiled for a variety of reasons. Some firms gave commemorative gifts to employees for long service. For example, Crossley's of Halifax recorded all employees who had given more than forty years service in 1954. Fielden Brothers of Todmorden gave New Year gifts to all personnel between 1853 and 1857, the list being arranged by job not name. This firm also offered help during a smallpox epidemic and listed all those employees who were affected by the disease. In 1861 the company provided a pension of 2s a week to their 'old handloom weavers'.

2.5 Apprenticeships

From the thirteenth century onwards most trades and professions required a formal apprenticeship called an indenture for their members. Boys, and often girls, were legally bound to serve a master for a fixed term in return for training, board and lodgings, though later some apprentices found their own board and lodgings. This system

Enquiry of long service for Tomkinson and Adam Ltd, dated 1931, Carpet Museum Trust.

was reinforced by the Statute of Apprentices of 1563, which banned anyone from practising a trade without proper apprenticeship.

From this time until the mid-nineteenth century many pauper children were apprenticed out to local employers and a great many still further afield. Sending children from the southern counties to the northern mills was an easy way of shifting the burden from one parish to another.

After the 1802 Health and Morals of Apprentices Act, better records had to be kept of parish apprentices, though as this was not enforced by the law it was not always followed. Two copies of the indentures were drawn up and signed by the child's parent or guardian and the master. Each then kept a copy of the indenture and this may have survived in personal records. A small number of individual indentures may be found in county record offices.

Todmorden Town Hall, West Yorkshire, opened in 1875.

Records for 'poor-law' apprentices frequently survive as loose sheets or in a register of parish apprentices and include the name of apprentice, date of indenture, age, parents' names (if known), name of person to whom they were apprenticed, their trade and term of apprenticeship.

The agreement between apprentice and master could only be broken legally by the Justices of the Peace and then only in serious circumstances, such as abuse or ill-treatment. These cases will be found in Quarter Sessions records. Some apprentices also did not complete the training. With the growth of the factory system apprenticeships became less used and the system eventually died out.

Many record offices have now transcribed apprentice indentures or indexed them. For example, Bury Archives has online lists from 1675 to 1836, an example being that of George Heywood, 14, son of Thomas Heywood, who was apprenticed to Joseph Pearson of Freetown, a hatter, on 28 April 1825.

A famous group of apprentices were based at Quarry Bank Mill at Styal, Cheshire. Like other mills in the area, a special apprentice house was built here for the children who came from Staffordshire, South

Apprenticeship indenture, Knaresborough, 1733.

Cheshire, Liverpool, London and East Anglia. The Register of Apprentices, along with other business records, is at the Central Library in Manchester.

The early mills often used pauper apprentices, including some from London. Records for these may be found in the London Parish records such as at City of Westminster Archives or London Metropolitan Archives and local poor-law records. Some parishes were sufficiently concerned to send inspectors to see what sort of conditions the children lived in and the inspectors' reports were sometimes published in London newspapers. One such report, into the cotton mills of John, Thomas and Samuel Haigh in Marsden, Huddersfield, appeared in the *European Magazine and London Review* in September 1798 (Aspin, *The Water Spinners*). The Haighs took in over eighty apprentices between 1792 and 1803.

2.5.1 Apprenticeship books

Between 1710 and 1811 stamp duty became payable on apprenticeships and Commissioners of Stamps kept registers of the money they

Apprentices House, Quarry Bank, Styal, Cheshire.

received from the duty paid. Some may be found in county record offices but the bulk of them are in The National Archives in series IR1. Since payment did not have to be made until twelve months after the date of the indenture, it may be necessary to search records for a number of years.

The apprenticeship books record the names, addresses and trades of the masters, names of the apprentices, dates of their indentures and names of the apprentices' parents, at least up to 1752. If the stamp duty was paid in London, entries are in the 'City' registers in the series; where it was paid elsewhere, entries are in the 'Country' registers; both registers are arranged in date order. There are personal-name indexes for both masters from 1710 to 1762 and apprentices from 1710 to 1774 on microfiche.

The masters and apprentices indexes are held at the Society of Genealogists, and a further set of copies are in London's Guildhall Library and The National Archives at Kew, as well as being online at British Origins: www.originsnetwork.com/BOWelcome.aspx.

Correspondence and minutes about the apprenticeship of pauper children can be found in poor-law records at local record offices.

Some apprentices were undertaken without any formal documentation. Children simply learned the trade from their parents.

2.6 Photographs

Businesses took photographs for promotional purposes or of specific events, such as centenaries or the opening of a new mill, and these sometimes show employees in their departments or working on machinery. Unfortunately, it is rare that a full list of names accompanies such images.

2.7 Inventory of stock

The business needed to know the value of its stock and also how much was in a completed state and how much partially finished in the loom. These inventories provide names of workers (again often just surnames) and show the value and/or length of cloth being woven.

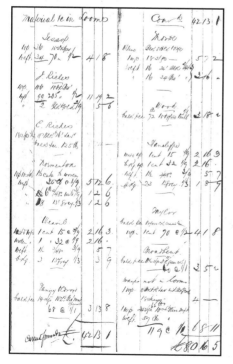

Inventory of stock, Glendinning Brothers, Huddersfield, 1870s.

2.8 Disputes

Disputes between worker and employer were usually reported in the newspaper, but take some searching for as they are not indexed. You really need to know that something of the nature of what took place or be very lucky. Disputes over completing work or being paid for it often ended up in the local court. If this was the case, the full details will appear in the newspaper, giving names of the parties, evidence given and the verdict.

On 7 September 1867 it was reported that James Whareham, weaver, of Oakes, Huddersfield, had claimed £1 11s 7d (£1.58) for work done for Messrs Liddell and Martin, manufacturers. Apparently he had woven a piece for the firm, brought it in on 17 August and was then told that they were going to stop part of his wages for a piece he'd woven in June, which had been passed at the time but was now found to be faulty. Whareham argued that the damage must have been done after he had handed the piece in. In this case, the weaver won and was awarded the amount claimed and his costs.

General disputes that involved a greater number of workers may not give individual names but simply record the event and the outcome. The Ministry of Labour was established in 1916 and was responsible for employment, industrial relations and health and safety. LAB2 contains surviving correspondence of the Ministry of Labour, and its

Strikers, Cleator Mill, Cumbria, 1915.

predecessors, prior to 1933. After 1933 the records are arranged into a number of different series, details of which can be found in The National Archives guides. LAB10 contains records relating to the Ministry's responsibility for industrial relations. LAB3 deals with those relating specifically to arbitration.

2.9 Union records

The nineteenth century saw the growth of trade unions. As people increasingly came together to work in factories, they began to realise that by banding together they could put pressure on employers to increase wages or improve working conditions. Cotton unions were among the earliest. A 'labour aristocracy' began to emerge, seeing a greater influence in politics and in health and safety at work. Eventually, out of this movement, the Labour Party developed (see Places to Go section – The People's History Museum in Manchester). In 1776, the Stocking Makers' Association for Mutual Protection became the first group to try to represent workers in the knitting industry. In 1812 the Union Society of Framework Knitters tried to establish a minimum pay rate, although it was not successful. It eventually expanded, with members throughout the Midlands and even London.

Some of the earliest unions were among the spinners, particularly in Lancashire, where the first one was established in Stockport in 1785. Many of these unions also offered friendly society benefits to their members.

However, under the Combination Laws of 1799 and 1800 prosecutions were made much easier and trade unions were often driven underground, though some societies reformed unofficially during major strikes. The laws were repealed in 1824 but almost immediately a number of strikes followed, leading to the Combination Act of 1825, which gave a very narrow definition of what a trade union was allowed to do – merely bargain about wages and conditions. They were specifically banned from 'molesting', 'obstructing' or 'intimidating' others. These words, of course, were open to the interpretation of the judge, who generally had more in common with the employers than the workers. This did not stop the growth of individual trade or craft unions but these groups soon realised that a wider membership base would be even more effective. Women also became involved. In 1915 250 women went on strike at Cleator Mills, Cumbria, successfully winning a war bonus for their work.

The complexity of union history is well illustrated in tracing two of the largest unions with textile sections.

In 1852 the Friendly Association of Hand Mule Spinners was formed in Preston, Lancashire, drawing its membership not just from Lancashire but from the neighbouring areas of Cheshire, Derbyshire and Yorkshire. By 1870 this had grown into the Amalgamated Association of Operative Cotton Spinners, and had a national membership.

The following year the Amalgamated Operative Dyers' Accident, Burial and Trade Protection Society was formed in Bradford. Just six years later this closed but formed the basis of the Amalgamated Society of Dyers (ASD), created in 1878. Further branches were opened in the surrounding towns, such as Macclesfield and Leeds.

The National Federation of Bleachers, Dyers and Kindred Trades, founded in 1896, looked after workers in the dyeing and finishing industries and had over 10,000 members. It was dissolved in 1920.

In 1936 the Amalgamated Society of Dyers, Bleachers, Finishers and Kindred Trades, the National Union of Textile Workers and the Operative Bleachers, Dyers and Finishers Association (Bolton Amalgamation) joined together to form the National Union of Dyers, Bleachers and Textile Workers (NUDBTW). The decline in the textile industry and in union membership generally precipitated the amalgamation of many unions and the NUDBTW became part of the Transport and General Workers' Union (T&G) in 1982. This led to the formation of the textiles trade group of the T&G, and represented the largest union in the British textile industry. The T&G is itself now part of Unite, formed in 2007.

The other large union is the General, Municipal, Boilermakers and Allied Trades Union (GMB). Smaller unions have gradually merged with this giant, including the Amalgamated Textile Workers, the United Garment Workers Union (from 1912), which itself was formed by a merger of the Amalgamated Society of Journeymen Tailors, Amalgamated Union of Clothiers' Operatives, Amalgamated Jewish Tailors, Pressers and Machinists' Trade Union, London Clothiers Cutters, the Shirt, Jacket and Overall Workers, the Belfast Shirt and Collar Workers, Scottish National Association of Operative Tailors, London Operative Tailors and the Amalgamated Society of Tailors and Tailoresses. In 1931 this group merged with the United Ladies Tailors (London) and Waterproof Garment Workers' Union to form the National Union of Tailors and Garment Workers, which became a member of the GMB in 1991.

Most areas had their own branches of the trade union, and most jobs within textiles had their own type of union, such as the Accrington District Card and Blowing Room Operatives and Ring Spinners Association or the Liverpool Flagmen's Friendly Society. However, some unions in the textile industry were very local (often one town, sometimes one factory or mill) and very specific in the type of worker they organised – and these unions were often quite short-lived. Although millions of workers joined unions, even by the end of the nineteenth century only one in ten employees was a member. While a massive volume of documents has survived, the records of many unions and most union members have long since been lost. An excellent website, run by Mark Crail, lists many unions that have been in existence in Britain and gives suggestions for further research. It is well worth a visit and can be accessed at: www.unionancestors.co.uk/. Other sources include:

• The National Archives – Parliamentary Papers have some trade-union information, mainly relating to the changes in laws concerning workers' associations, trade unions and trade-union activity. FS1–4 is the main series of Friendly Society rules (1784–1912), but only FS2 and FS4 are indexed (by place).

Christine Shepherd with Norman Willis MP in Geneva.

• The Home Office and Treasury Solicitor's Office – records contain some information about trade unions prior to 1850. Legal records may also be useful since the earlier unions were illegal. Series HO41, HO45 and HO144 contain material relating to union activity that was seen as particularly militant or illegal after 1850.

• FS12 (1872–1958) – contains the annual returns for registered trade unions where you may find such information as: name of individual union, numbers in the union (and any change during the previous year), branch status (whether it is a branch of a regional/national union), political affiliation, names/addresses of individual union officers, income and financial position, comments on disputes or short working. These records are listed by place name and can be easily searched.

• Many local (branch) records can be found in the appropriate county or borough record offices. The online indexes of National Register of Archives contain a mass of information about the location of trade-union and friendly society records. For national (and some local) records of trade unions, as well as those of the TUC, researchers should begin their search at the Modern Records Centre, Warwick, but also search A2A Access to Archives catalogue.

The records themselves are a mixed bunch. Some provide extensive details, while others list only a surname. For example, a register from the Huddersfield & Dewsbury Powerloom Tuners Society, 1860–1996, has a section for each company at which members were employed. The number of looms worked is given followed by a list of members engaged there as tuners.

2.9.1 Membership books

These generally give full details with names and addresses or places of work, but some, especially early ones, are just a list of who paid subs. Some may also give details of transfers to other branches on change of employment. During boom years, many workers changed jobs frequently and so would also often need to be enrolled at a different branch of their union.

2.9.2 Out-of-work benefits

Membership brought more than just support for a strike. If workers fell on hard times, they would often receive a small pay out from their union and records of this may have been kept, again listing names, dates and amount paid out. It is, though, useful to search through such records to see when people were in or out of work as this may provide the clue to explain why an ancestor moved house – perhaps to a cheaper area or to take up employment elsewhere.

2.9.3 Funeral benefits

Often a grant would be made for funeral expenses, sometimes to the widow for the worker themselves, but payments might also be made for the death of a child or wife. These details are useful as they provide an indication of date of death, which can then be followed up in death or burial registers.

2.9.4 Officers of the union

The more prominent your ancestor was in the union, the more likely you are to find references to them. Someone had to collect the weekly subs and write up the register. Also, there was generally a 'union rep' at each mill and many were sent on courses to learn more about speaking for their members or to represent the union at national or even international level. For example, after Christine Shepherd became a representative for the Dyers and Bleachers and Textile Workers in Huddersfield she was invited to go to an international conference in Geneva. These are the people who will be mentioned in the union records.

2.9.5 Branch records

These generally comprise membership information, details of the representatives in each of the mills or factories, correspondence, notebooks and minute books. Financial books and accounts rarely give much genealogical detail.

2.9.6 Minute books

These record the events and decisions made at a meeting, as well as all the people who attended the meeting – or who sent apologies for not attending. Meetings could include branch meetings, shop steward's meetings and works committees (committees organised by the employer, such as Health & Safety), which included union reps, employers and trades councils. Members, particularly officers of the branch, may be referred to by name but may also simply be referred to as 'representative of . . .' a named mill. Minutes are rarely indexed and are only really of use if you know your ancestor was involved in the union at a particular date. Even then they may only confirm this involvement, though you may be lucky and find more information.

2.9.7 Correspondence

This may include letters sent by the union reps to employers, often of a general nature but also relating to specific disputes and will then name the individuals concerned. Letters were also sent to other unions and to local reps. You might be lucky and find copies of letters sent and also copies of replies, so be able to follow the full story. Alternatively you find half the story and have to 'fill in' the rest for yourself. These sort of records may have a general index (i.e., letters to firms beginning with A filed under A but not strict alphabetical order), they may be in date order or may not be indexed at all.

2.9.8 Strikes

Strikes generated many papers, but do not always mention individuals, except perhaps the union reps. The businesses affected, number of workers on strike, together with the cause and progress of the dispute, can make a fascinating background to your family history, though. Further information can be found at The National Archives Ministry of Labour records (see p. 42).

Chapter 3

SOURCES FOR OWNERS

Generally more records relating to ownership of businesses survive than those for workers, partly because more were generated.

3.1.1 Business records

Any business has to begin trading and this involves keeping some sort of paperwork. Even a sole trader must keep some financial records, though these may be of little genealogical value. With partnerships, two or more people may set up a business together with no legal documentation at all. Sometimes a notice was inserted in the newspapers to state that 'John Smith and Sam Jones are now in partnership'. However, legal ties are established by the very fact of trading together and these are more difficult to break, bringing also the danger of liability for another's actions. Many, therefore, set up a more formal agreement known as a deed of partnership.

3.1.2 Deed of partnership

These name all the partners, place of residence and occupation and give details of name and purpose of the company formed. In February 1837 Joseph Bell Clarke of Manchester, cotton manufacturer, William Edward Acraman, Alfred John Acraman, Philip William Skynner Miles, Thomas Kington, Peter Maze, George Gibbs, Robert Bright, Charles Pinney, Robert Edward Case, George Henry Ames, Richard Ricketts, Frederick Ricketts and Henry Bush, merchants, and Peter Freeland Aiken, banker, all of Bristol, James George, esq, Mayor of Bristol, Daniel Cave and Joseph Cookson of Bristol, esq, all went into partnership to form Clarke Acramans Maze & Co. in order to start a manufactory for spinning and weaving cotton around Bristol with Joseph Clarke as Chairman and Peter Maze as Deputy Chairman.

Any changes to the partnership, such as death or retirement of a partner, taking on of another partner or changing the purpose of the business, must all be accompanied by further deeds. By October 1837 William Edward Acraman and Alfred J Acraman decided to leave the partnership and so two deeds were created dissolving the existing partnership and assigning their shares to the continuing partners. One of these deeds also gives further details of Joseph Clarke, describing him as 'late of Manchester, now of Arno Court, Somerset'. Eventually the name of the company became the Great Western Cotton Works, but this was still a partnership so when Joseph Clarke retired from the business, a further deed was created setting out the arrangements on his retirement and the admission of his son, Henry George Clarke, as partner (Bristol Record office ref 12142/1).

As all partners are liable for the debts of the company, just as sole traders are liable for their own debts, in the event of the partnership ceasing or expanding, it is important to inform everyone of the fact.

Ending a partnership is known as 'dissolving' the agreement. Not only must legal documents be drawn up for this, but notices also appear in the newspapers to ensure that all customers understand what is happening. Once the partnership is ended, the partners are no longer responsible for each other's debts. Notices also give details of any further business any or all of the partners become involved with. This is also the case when a new partner is taken into the group. These notices are not indexed and they are not necessarily 'full-page spreads' so are not easy to find. An approximate date of dissolution of the partnership is needed.

3.1.3 Bankruptcy

When a sole trader or partnership ceases trading because they cannot pay their debts, the people involved become bankrupt, either voluntarily, when a person petitions for their own bankruptcy, or involuntarily, when a creditor petitions for a debtor's bankruptcy.

The Bankruptcy Act of 1571 allowed for Commissioners of bankrupts to be appointed to manage the bankrupt's financial affairs and to enable the bankrupt to pay as much of the debts as possible. Once the distribution of assets had been agreed and the portion of the debt paid off, the bankrupt could start trading again. Originally only traders could be declared bankrupt. Others were known as insolvent debtors and could be jailed for non-payment of debts. Not surprisingly, people often lied about their exact occupation so as to qualify as a trader and not be sent to a debtors' prison. Most bankruptcy records don't survive, but those that do can be found at The National Archives in the 'B' letter code:

- B1 – records relating to unsettled cases or appeals.
- B3 – surviving case files from 1759 to 1911, indexed by name.
- B4 Docket Books – chronological registers of commissions and fiats from 1710 to 1849 but are incomplete.
- B5 – some enrolments of commissions and fiats after 1758. Appointments of Full-time Official Assignees (who were appointed to value the assets of the debtor), 1832–1855; some Certificates of Conformity and details of transfer of assets to trustees.
- B6 – registers of petitions for Adjudication in Bankruptcy, 1849–1869; indexed Registers of Certificates of Conformity for 1733–1817 and deposited Certificates for 1815–1856. These give the name of the bankrupt, his address and the date the Certificate was issued. The Certificate discharged him from any remaining debt. Registers of Petitions for Bankruptcy from 1870 to 1883; registers relating to London Court cases, 1861–1870.
- B7 – further records relating to unsettled cases or appeals.
- B8 – indexes from 1820 onwards.
- B9 – case files after 1832, but after 1869 the files mainly refer to London area.
- B10 – case files from 1858–1862.

LCO28 (Lord Chancellor's Office) records include some Registers of Petitions for protection from bankruptcy process in county court cases, from 1854. Further legal actions against bankrupts may also be found in the records of other courts – Chancery, Exchequer, King's Bench and Common Pleas.

Very early commissions of bankruptcy may be found in the Patent Rolls (C66 – C67); conveyances of bankrupts' estates are enrolled on the Close Rolls (C54) and relevant petitions are sometimes found in the State Papers (SP).

It was important that bankruptcy was advertised as widely as possible so the Commissioners published notices in the *London Gazette* (The National Archives records ZJ1). Many of these notices date back to the seventeenth century and are indexed after 1789. These are now available online in a fully searchable version at: www.gazettes-

Extract from the Leeds Mercury, *1817, showing the name, town and occupation of bankrupts listed in the* London Gazette.

online.org.uk. They include some bankruptcies that do not appear in the B class records. Other newspapers also included these bankruptcy notices, principally *The Times*, but local papers also carried the information.

In the earlier newspapers the details appear in paragraph form, so be prepared to read the page in detail to find the information you require:

> Whereas a Commission of Bankrupt is awarded and issued forth against John Woolford the Younger, of Ipswich in the County of Suffolk, Sacking Weaver, Dealer and Chapman, and he being declared a Bankrupt, is hereby required to surrender himself to the Commissioners in the said Commission named, or the major Part of them, on the 4th, 11th and 27th of November next, at Four o'clock in the afternoon, on each of the said Days, at Guildhall, London, and make a full Discovery and disclosure of his Estate and Effects when and where his Creditors are to come prepared to prove their Debts, and at the Second Sitting to chose Assignees,

and at the last Sitting the said Bankrupt is required to finish his Examination, and the Creditors are to assent to or dissent from the Allowance of his Certificate. All Persons indebted to the said Bankrupt, or that have any of his Effects, are not to pay or deliver the same but to whom the Commissioners shall appoint, but give Notice to Messrs Benn, attorneys, in Pudding Lane, London

From the *London Gazette*, Issue 9626, published on the 12 October 1756

The following month a notice informed creditors when the final dividend would be paid.

Later issues give the information in the form of a table, which is much easier to follow and it is possible to track the details from beginning to end.

When William Mortimer of Wakefield petitioned for bankruptcy the *London Gazette* of 4 September 1891 published details of a 'Receiving Order'. Information included his name and address – both his residence and trading addresses – occupation, court at which the hearing would be held (generally in the nearest town), date the petition was filed and of the receiving order, index number allocated to the case and whether the petition was made by the creditors or, as in this case, the debtor himself. Knowing in which court the hearing is held can suggest other sources – the local newspaper will probably report the case or papers may be available in the local record office.

On 11 September notice of the first meeting was published, repeating the basic details but also including the time, date and place of the first meeting together with the time, date and place of public examination. After this trustees would be appointed who would then collect together all the assets available. A Notice of Intended Dividend was published on 27 November 1891, followed by a Notice of Dividends (indicating what was actually going to be paid) on 1 January 1892. Once these were agreed, Mortimer then applied for an Application for Discharge, which shows a date for the court hearing and was published in the *London Gazette* on 11 October 1892. This was followed on 13 December 1892 by publication of an Orders Made on Application for Discharge; Mortimer's discharge was delayed for two years, until sufficient debt had been paid off. Once this was settled, the trustees had to be 'released' from their obligations. Notice of Release of Trustees appeared on 12 May 1893.

In 1842 District Bankruptcy Courts were set up, but from 1869 bankruptcy was dealt with in the county courts and records will be found in the local county record offices.

After 1883, the London Court of Bankruptcy became part of the Supreme Court as the High Court of Justice in Bankruptcy, but petitions were only heard here if the debtor lived in London or had a business there, if he didn't live in England or if the creditors could not find out where he lived. High Court judges could also transfer cases from county courts.

After 1861 insolvent debtors could also petition for bankruptcy. However, some people who had been traders may have been treated as insolvent debtors so their records too may appear and these may give even more details. At Wakefield courthouse on 17 October 1840 the case of Jacob Moore was heard. The following extract from the *London Gazette* gives his working history:

> late of Sparkethead, near Bradford, Yorkshire Worsted Top-Maker and Manufacturer, now out of business then of same place, Beer-Seller, previously of Northowram near Halifax, Yorkshire, then of Hamburgh, Germany, Merchant and Commission Agent, then of Northowram aforesaid, Worsted Top-Maker, then traveller for Joseph Stocks and Company, Ale and Porter Brewers, in Northowram aforesaid, and formerly of same place, Woolstapler, Dealer in Noils* and Worsted Waste, having a Warehouse in Gaol Lane, Halifax aforesaid.

*Noils are the short fibres left after combing to separate them from the long fibres before spinning into yarn.

3.1.4 Limited liability companies

An alternative to partnerships was a company. Previously expensive and time-consuming to set up because an individual Act of Parliament was needed, a law that came into force on 1 November 1844 allowed the formation of a company, having more than twenty-five members, by simple registration. The Registrar of Joint Stock Companies (later called the Registrar of Companies) was responsible for registering all companies in England. Personal liability for the company's debts remained until the Limited Liability Act 1855.

Files kept by the Registrar of Companies are for all companies currently in existence and for twenty years after their demise. After this files may have been destroyed or been transferred to The National Archives:

- BT41 – registrations under the 1844 Act are arranged in alphabetical order by the company title and may include name and address of the business, its solicitors and its promoters, together with a prospectus, the purpose of the business and financial details, such as capital and number of shares.
- BT31 – registrations from 1856 onwards, but there is some overlap until 1860. These are in order of company number. From 1955 records are arranged by date of dissolution.
- BT34 – accounts filed by liquidators from 1890 to 1932.
- BT95 – index giving brief details of dissolved companies whose papers have been destroyed; arranged by date of incorporation.

The main index to company numbers is held by Companies Registration Office, Companies House, Crown Way, Maindy, Cardiff, CF14 3UZ; email: enquiries@companies-house.gov.uk; tel: 0870 3333636. It is available online at: www.companies-house.gov.uk. Companies House also has details of current companies and these can be purchased online.

There is a card index to companies dissolved before 1963, but this is only available in the Cardiff Search Room. Requests for information can be made by post, telephone, fax or email. Each card indicates whether the file has been destroyed or transferred to The National Archives, in which case it will be marked with the box number in BT31, as well as the company number and the date of dissolution.

The National Archives has indexes to help you find company registration numbers. Names are in alphabetical order by legal title, so John Crossley & Sons of Halifax will be found under 'J' not 'C', as you would expect. There are some later indexes on microfiche.

The National Archives website gives full details of the background to the Registration of Companies and Businesses with links to the various sections under which the records are held.

The Historical Manuscripts Commission (now part of The National Archives) has published guides to some of the manuscripts held at The National Archives. Included in the 'Guides to Sources for British History' Series is *Records of British business and industry 1760–1914: textiles and leather*, published in 1990.

Business Archives Council

This organisation exists to encourage the study and safeguarding of business archives. It regularly publishes articles on the subject but has no archives that can be consulted. It may, however, be able to help with tracing the whereabouts of business archives. The BAC's collection of business histories is now at the Centre for Business History in Scotland, University of Glasgow. More about the work of the Council can be found at: www.businessarchivescouncil.org.uk/.

3.1.5 Prospectuses

These invite people to subscribe but little further information is included, except names of the proposers of the company. Some of these will be lodged with company papers in local record offices, and occasionally at The National Archives or the Guildhall Library, London.

3.1.6 Memorandum and Articles of Association

These are formal documents setting out the purpose and rules of the company. These also give the names and addresses of directors and how shares will be allocated.

3.1.7 Share books

Many of these have survived, and are usually in the local record office. These registers give an index number, name of shareholder, address of shareholder, how many shares held and when/how many transferred and to whom – this may often be either to a relative or to a solicitor/trustee in the event of death. Any changes of address are shown, provided the company has been informed.

The shareholders may have been local but could just as well have come from further afield. The Heckmondwike Manufacturing Company share register shows shareholders from Scarborough, Harrogate and Blackpool, who are likely to have been local businesspeople who had retired to those towns, but other addresses included Worksop, Darlington, Andover, London and even overseas. Henry Moor Bell of 2157 51st Ave West, Vancouver, Canada, held fifty shares, which in December 1932 were transferred: fourteen each going to Henry Trevitt of Heckmondwike, manager, Arthur Wilson of Heckmondwike, colliery manager, and Auberon Herbert Redfearn of

Liversedge, solicitor, while eight went to Alfred Charles Morton of Heckmondwike, secretary and cashier.

3.1.8 Register of directors

These registers give details of directors, including addresses and number of shares held. Changes to directors will also be found here.

3.1.9 Co-operative

The Co-operative Movement sprang up in the nineteenth century and this was applied to company ownership too, particularly around Oldham where many mills were built and run by joint-stock companies, often called the 'Oldham Limiteds'. The shareholders were not the wealthy but the wage-earning workers. For example, the Sun Mill Company was set up in about 1859. Existing records, which can be found at the John Rylands Library, Manchester, include minute books for the board of directors, shareholders' ledgers and registers, visitors' book and newspaper cuttings relating to the mill.

This trend spread elsewhere, for example, Queen Street Mill in Burnley. Now a museum, it was built at the end of the nineteenth century as a workers co-operative.

3.1.10 Financial records

These records will include balance sheets, profit and loss accounts and so on. They give fascinating background to the company but are of little genealogical value. Details of suppliers, carriers and customers may enable you to plot the geographical spread of business dealings and suggest where, or why, ancestors might have moved, but this is rather tenuous.

3.1.11 Deeds or indentures

Deeds are simply legal agreements, for example, leases of property, mortgages on mills, deeds of apprenticeship and so on. They give details of the parties involved, their occupation and residence. They will often refer to previous deeds relating to property and give details of generations, especially when a person dies and their share is passed on and split between members of the family.

3.1.12 Fire insurance

After the Great Fire of London in 1666 a number of fire-insurance offices came into existence, initially in London and later throughout the country. By the late eighteenth century, most towns in England and Wales had an agent linked to one of the large London fire-insurance companies. These were not only necessary from the point of view of insurance, but they also often provided the only fire brigade – and they would only attend fires for their own clients.

Many of the records of these companies are held at the Guildhall Library in London, though only a few have policy registers surviving. Ones that do include: the Hand-in-Hand Company, which operated mainly in London, 1696–1865; the Sun Fire Insurance, 1710–1863; and the Royal Exchange, 1753–1759, 1773–1883. There are a few surviving policy registers for the Globe, Law Union and Rock, London and Lancashire, and London Assurance. No policy registers seem to have survived for the Phoenix Insurance company, whose records are held at Cambridge University Library, not the Guildhall Library. Those that do survive will probably contain:

- The policy number, premium, renewal date and some details of endorsements (usually special conditions or changes to policy details). Endorsements on Sun policy registers are in a series of 168 endorsement books, which survive for 1728–1865, reference number Ms 12160 at the Guildhall Library. Sun fire-insurance policies were renewable after five years when a policy was issued under a new number.
- names of the agent and/or location of the agency.
- names, status, occupation and address of policyholder.
- names, occupations and addresses of tenants if the property were leased.
- location, type, nature of construction and value of property insured.

Online indexes exist for policies issued by the Sun Fire Insurance office between 1808 and 1835. You can search them at: www.a2a.org.uk. More information about the records can be found at: www.history. ac.uk/gh/sun.htm. Although most policies were issued for companies in London, there are many policies for provincial firms, such as the one issued in November 1833 for 'John Ormerod and Sons, Bankside near Rochdale Lancaster, wool spinners and manufacturers'.

Some individual fire-insurance policies will be found at the local record office. These may be with the records of the business, but may also be found in solicitors' or estate agents' records. The policy for Upper Houghton Mill, for example, can be found in the Lancashire Record Office at Preston in the records of Houghton, Craven and Co. of Preston, solicitors.

Insurance brokers' records may also include references to fire-insurance policies.

3.1.13 Goad fire-insurance maps

Some local record offices or libraries also hold copies of Goad fire-insurance and shopping-centre maps for their own area. These were produced between 1885 and 1970 for many towns and cities in the British Isles and usually have a scale of 1in to 40ft or 50ft. All buildings and businesses in each street are shown and revisions were produced every five or six years. A comprehensive set of Goad maps and insurance plans can be found at the British Library.

3.1.14 Company minute books

These often do survive since they are legal documents recording decisions made by the Board of Directors. The books are in date order and each meeting begins with a list of those present, often accompanied by apologies for absence. The main points of the discussion are recorded, often giving details of who made the remarks, together with decisions taken and voting results if applicable. These give a good insight into how the business was run, how and why decisions were made and sometimes suggest reasons for splits in the firm.

3.1.15 Letters

Outgoing correspondence was often kept in a 'letter book'. The very earliest entries are likely to be handwritten using copying ink. Once completed, the still-damp letter would be pressed onto flimsy paper to obtain a copy. The reason for using such flimsy paper is that the copy is 'in reverse' so the paper has to be thin enough to allow the ink to show through. Later, typed letters had a carbon copy. Letters will generally be listed in date order but will often have a basic, initial letter index, which you will need to read through to see if any relevant firm is mentioned. Incoming correspondence may be kept, but rarely survives in great numbers. Some may have been stored in letter books, or boxes, again in date order but with some sort of index.

Often you will find tantalising glimpses of business dealings but not be able to follow it through to the final outcome. In April 1884 Thomas Brierley of Denby Dale wrote a very indignant letter to Jonas Kenyon & Sons:

> yours of the 4th is now before me and is such, I suppose as you have been accustomed to with Messrs Littlewood. Allow me to tell you it is at all times a great pleasure to us to oblige our customers 'great or small' but certainly object to be dictated to by you and in such a manner as you think fit. We existed a long time since without your assistance or insults and can do again.

Unfortunately the letter that sparked this indignation is now lost, nor is the reply on record. However, the two firms were still doing business later in the year so must have reached some agreement eventually.

Although letters may have little direct genealogical value, they show which other companies the firm was doing business with. It is also possible to track the progress of managers to see their day-to-day working life or discover which dates they worked at the firm. You may also find an original signature of your ancestor, if you are prepared for a long search.

3.1.16 Letter headings

These often feature a fairly accurate engraving of the mill and any other branch addresses, which may suggest further research areas if an ancestor has moved away.

3.1.17 Patents

From the sixteenth century the Crown granted monopolies for specific trades, inventions or manufacturers, including the sale of specific goods such as silks. After considerable abuse of the system, it fell into disfavour but continued to be developed through the courts. By the eighteenth century it was a condition of a grant of patent that a full description of the invention and its use had to be supplied. In 1785 Richard Arkwright fell foul of this requirement when he failed to supply a sufficient specification and his patent for his spinning machine became void, thus allowing others to develop and use it without payment to him. It was James Watt's patent for steam engines and subsequent court cases that established the principle that further patents could be granted for improvements (by another inventor) to existing machines.

The Patent Office was established in 1852. This simplified procedures and reduced fees, as well as introducing a single patent publication for all parts of Britain, making it easier for the less wealthy to apply for patents. Further Acts of 1883 and 1902 introduced and extended the idea of actually examining the invention for its effectiveness and novelty. This entailed extensive searching in previous patents, thus encouraging a system of classification. Details were arranged in volumes under subject and given a unique number.

Copies of patents can be found at the British Library, Science Reference Library, 96 Euston Road, London NW1 2DB. Information about their holdings can be found on their website: www.bl.uk/collections/patents.html.

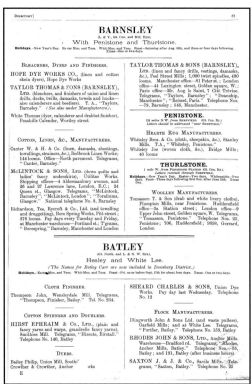

Extract from the Textile Directory, *Yorkshire, 1911.*

Records prior to 1852 are published works such as indexes, which give brief details. Originals are held at The National Archives. The information at The National Archives comprises:

- Printed indexes – these are held in the Map Room, indexed by name of inventor, date of patent and by the type of invention.
- SP44 State Papers Domestic – petitions to the Crown for patents before 1782, with entry books of petitions from 1661.
- HO42, HO43, HO44 and HO45 Home Office records – records of patents from 1782.
- LO1 Law Officers reports – includes some applications by patent agents and disputed cases, 1839–1885.

The patents include the names of the inventor and associates and details of the invention itself. A useful guide can be found at: www. nationalarchives.gov.uk/catalogue/RdLeaflet.asp?sLeafletID=77&j=1.

3.1.18 Solicitors

Frequently the collections from solicitors' firms have been deposited and kept together, so it is worth checking to see if there is something relating to a particular business or investment. Disputes with neighbouring businesses, with employees or the local council required the support of a legal advisor. Disputes could include court cases involving theft of cloth, disputes over watercourses or supply of water or fraud on the part of an employee. These may or may not be indexed. Some are merely collections of correspondence, but others may include deeds or leases, copies of wills, details of family disputes, plans and records of building purchases and reference to patents or partnerships.

3.1.19 Estate agents

Involved in the buying and selling of property, estate agents' records may include plans of the buildings or surrounding area, full descriptions of the property, including any mill machinery in the deal, and sometimes a brief history of the mill. Sale catalogues usually covered machinery or auctions of cloth or yarn.

3.1.20 Employers' associations

Some employers' associations go back to the beginning of the nineteenth century, formed as a response to the increasing workers' associations and unions. The majority of records are, though, likely to be later nineteenth century and often consist of broad-ranging agreements or pamphlets on wage levels, conditions at work or committee work. There may also be some archival material that is of more genealogical value, but little is indexed. Examples include the Oldham and Rochdale Textile Employers' Association, the West of England Wool Textile Employers' Association or the Colne & Holme Valley's Mill Owners' & Occupiers' Association.

Records may include: minute books, details of agreements (or disputes) between employers' associations and unions or workers' associations, correspondence or letter books, press cuttings, national or local agreements regarding wage levels and membership lists.

3.1.21 Trade directories

Starting from the end of the eighteenth century, these list prominent people in an area, give a description of the town and its environs and list tradespeople, often as an alphabetical list and also by trade. Just as with modern-day directories such as Yellow Pages or Thomson, entries had to be paid for so not all tradespeople were listed. Later directories are more informative.

Originals may be found in libraries or record offices, though many have now been produced in CD format for purchase. A useful website is maintained by the University of Leicester, and provides free access to trade directories in England and Wales and is searchable by location (county) or by decade (pre-1850s, then each decade up to 1910). It can be accessed at: www.historicaldirectories.org/.

Other trade directories may be specific to a product or trade or area, such as the *Yorkshire Textile Directory* or the *Cotton Spinners & Manufacturers' Directory of Lancashire. Yorkshire Industry and Commerce*, printed in 1893, gives an outline of industry (not just textiles) in some of the large towns in Yorkshire with illustrations of their mills, products and so on. Thomas Skinners' *Cotton Trade Directory of the World* illustrates the international quality of the textile trade. Companies and trade associations are indexed and there are lists of trademarks, directors, exporters and merchants. The directory also includes information about international production and lists of firms supplying mill furnishings.

Chapter 4

LIFE IN THE TEXTILE INDUSTRY

The raw materials for making fabric were originally organic – they came from plants or animals. To turn this material into a useful yarn required various processes, some of which are common to most fabrics, such as spinning and weaving, but some processes differ depending on what is being used and these are described in the appropriate chapter. The length of the fibre of the raw material, whether it is animal origin, such as wool, or vegetable origin, such as cotton or flax, is referred to as 'staple', for example 'long staple wool' or 'short staple cotton'.

From the earliest times, everyone who could tried to keep a few sheep for the wool that could be woven to make simple clothes for the family, or sold to merchants.

Dales sheep.

Spinning wheels at Dre-fach Felindre Museum.

The whole family was involved in the production of cloth. Even small children could help, using bats set with teasel heads to comb the wool before spinning. Spinning gives strength and produces yarn for weaving. At first, this process was done by hand in the home, producing single thread, usually by women, hence the term spinster as this was one of the few jobs respectable unmarried women could do. The women spun the wool, which would then be woven by the men. Weaving involves the interlacing of yarn to form a fabric. Warp threads (running the length of the cloth) are set up on the loom and the weft (running across the cloth) is passed back and forth, under and over the individual warp threads.

The cloth was too loosely woven to be used immediately and also still had some grease on it, which would prevent dyes taking properly. The cloth was washed to remove this grease, then scoured with water and an acidic cleaner such as stale urine or fuller's earth and pounded in the liquid, using large wooden hammers or by men trampling it in the vats. This gave rise to particular surnames, such as Walker, Fuller and Tucker – regional variations of the same occupational name. This process felted the material, thickening it and giving it strength. Fulling was the first textile process to be done in a mill. The earliest fulling mill known was mentioned in 1185 on Knights Templar's land at Temple Newsam, Leeds, but fulling mills were soon found wherever waterpower was available. The manor of Temple Wycombe, part of Wycombe Manor, also belonged to the Knights Templar, passing eventually to the Hospitallers of St John until the dissolution of the monasteries. Early Court Rolls and deeds relating to this, which mention fulling mills and their occupiers, are to be found at the Centre for Buckinghamshire Studies. Many fulling mills were later converted to spinning or weaving mills.

Other lords of the manor soon realised that this was another source of income, and therefore forced their tenants to take cloth to the lord's fulling mill. Records of the building and leasing of these mills often survive in estate records. Some lords built the mills themselves and then leased them, often to the same family through a number of generations. Others provided funds for mill building as a form of investment.

Some early fulling mills gradually expanded and developed over the years into the large-scale textile mills of the nineteenth century. In 1785 Joseph Sykes of Upper and Holt Mill, Slaithwaite, Huddersfield, asked Lord Dartmouth, one of the local landowners, for a loan of £100 to build a second scribbling mill. In 1790 Lord Dartmouth was asked for a further advance for a dyehouse at Lower Holt Mill. Upper Mill burnt down on 5 October 1805. Lower Holt Mill was taken over by J Varley and ultimately converted to a brewery. Some of the Dartmouth Estate records are deposited in the record office, others are kept at the estate offices in Slaithwaite.

The north and south of the country generally developed different systems for this cottage industry. In the north, raw material tended to be bought in small quantities and worked by individual families who

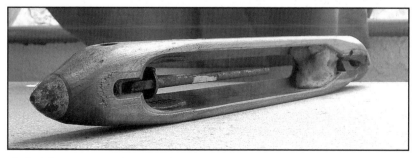

A shuttle.

often then sold a single piece of cloth to small clothiers who in turn could take it to market to sell to merchants. It is wrong, though, to assume that the title 'cloth manufacturer' in wills or deeds referred to very wealthy mill owner, as it did in later centuries. The manufacturers were initially more likely to be small-scale farmers who had sufficient capital to purchase a loom or two, with a spinning wheel. Raw material would be bought in from equally small-scale wool dealers (known as braggers) and the whole family would work together to produce the cloth. At this time there was no 'tie' to the dealer and the cloth could be sold to whoever offered the best price. Some managed to expand and 'put out' work to others in the area, either for spinning into yarn or weaving into cloth, or both, and then sell on the cloth.

In the south, the cottage workers generally received yarn from merchants who later collected the cloth to complete the process in finishing mills and take it to market. The cottagers had no choice in who they sold the cloth to since they did not buy the yarn themselves, but were paid to produce cloth by the merchants. This resulted in the wealth being created by a few men, while the bulk of the workers remained dependent on providing the labour for a small wage.

Whether produced in the home or in an early factory, the industry was still labour intensive. It took five or six spinners to produce

Spinning mule at Dre-fach Felindre Museum.

sufficient yarn for one weaver to complete one length of cloth. It was easier to transport the wool to the worker, hence the industry grew where people lived rather than where the sheep lived.

During the eighteenth century a series of inventions enabled all the cloth-making processes to be brought together in purpose-built factories. In 1733 John Kay invented his 'Flying Shuttle', which mechanised and improved the speed of weaving. Spinning improvements followed. James Hargreaves produced the 'Spinning Jenny' in 1764, followed in 1775 by Samuel Crompton's 'Mule', both of which increased yarn production. These machines were small enough to be used in the cottages or they could be power-driven, but it was the invention of Richard Arkwright's 'Spinning Frame' that saw the building of a large cotton mill in Cromford, Derbyshire, in 1771. This frame used water power to drive the machinery and Arkwright's invention became known as the 'Water Frame'. Workers were brought in from the surrounding areas, but young apprentices were often brought from much further afield, especially London. In 1786 Edmund Cartwright, who invented a power loom, had a cotton factory in Doncaster, until 1793 when it was abandoned and later sold. The invention of an automated loom speeded up the process of weaving. Joseph Jacquard (1752–1834) was born in France and developed a process of using punched cards to control the raising or lowering of warp threads, thus controlling the pattern being woven, in effect a very early computer. By the 1820s these were in widespread use. Often different yarns were used to produce different effects or properties of cloth, such as using a linen warp and cotton weft or including fancy wools such as alpaca in the weave.

There was a whole range of other inventions and developments, initially in the cotton industry, but which were quickly taken up and adapted by other branches of the textile business. The increase in productivity created by these inventions reduced the price of textiles considerably. It also led not only to the expansion of the industry, but also to massive social changes as people moved from the country into the towns and learned to become a 'workforce' that clocked on and off and worked predominately away from the home.

Children, who had always worked long hours at home, now worked long hours in the factories, too, often alongside their parents. In some instances, the children became the main breadwinners or made a substantial contribution to the family budget.

Starting with menial tasks, children crawled under machinery to clean out fluff and debris or twist together broken ends of yarn. The machinery was not stopped during this operation, leading to numerous accidents if the children were not sufficiently nimble. The mills also took on many pauper apprentices, often from long distances away from their families, but gradually pressure was exerted on the Government to bring in laws to protect young workers and with the introduction of compulsory education in 1870 child labour gradually ended.

A humid atmosphere was needed in the cotton mills, so employees often worked in damp clothes. Wool mills were drier but in both the fluff from the yarn hung in the atmosphere and was breathed in by the workers. The yarn and machinery also needed grease or oil to ensure they ran properly – textile mills have their own unique odour. Many workers became deaf after working for long hours in the weaving sheds, where hundreds of looms clattered non-stop. Even today, a textile mill is quite noisy, despite the improvements in machinery.

Cromford Mill was built in the Derbyshire countryside, and some were built on hillsides where water power was available. With the introduction of steam power, mills began to be built in the towns where transport on canals and rivers was easier and a labour force was easily found. These grew in size, from smaller three-storey mills to massive complexes. Later, these were powered by electricity and could then be

Beams at the back of a loom.

constructed anywhere in the country, though most stayed in traditional textile areas because the expertise already existed there.

Other processes included perching, or examining the woven cloth to detect any faults. The cloth was spread over rollers and the percher checked it, marking faults with chalk, ready for mending. The burler then had to remove any small impurities, bits of yarn and so on, with the aid of tiny 'burling irons' or tweezers. Highly skilled menders – who were always women – dealt with any faults such as loose or broken ends or small faults in the weave. The cloth could then be finished in various ways to make it usable. These processes may have included bleaching and dyeing, which could have been carried out by specialist industries or within the same factory.

Chapter 5

THE COTTON INDUSTRY

Very little cotton was worked in England before Tudor times, although the product was known and used in many other parts of the world. It requires warm weather to grow the plant, but a damp atmosphere to manufacture cotton yarn. Cotton appears to have been in use by the mid-seventeenth century, imported mainly from Cyprus and Syria. With the rise of the East India Company in the early eighteenth century came raw material and finished goods from India. A series of Calico Acts banning the import of cotton helped support home production of fustian, a mixture of wool or cotton and linen. When these Acts were eventually repealed in 1774 there had been sufficient innovation in methods of production to allow the English cotton industry to compete with India and eventually to overtake it.

In the early 1700s the cotton industry was home-based, but initially cotton had to be used just for the weft, with a linen warp, because then it was not possible to make cotton yarn strong enough for the warp. It was not until the late eighteenth century that all-cotton cloth could be made. After this, trade expanded considerably and many northern manufacturers had agents abroad. Transport improvements enabled large amounts of cotton to be brought in, principally from the colonies in America, often through the ports of Liverpool and Manchester. It was found that the damp atmosphere in the north west enabled cotton to be worked more easily. Coupled with an existing, well-established linen industry, this gave the impetus for the growth of the cotton industry in Lancashire – 'the cotton industry became more highly localised than any other contemporary manufacture in so far as it concentrated itself progressively within a third of a single county' (Farnie, *The English Cotton Industry*) – owing mainly to its damp climate, water supply, textile tradition, mechanical inventions, access to the markets and ports at Liverpool and Manchester and low transport costs. By mid-century, Manchester became known as 'Cottonopolis', though its manufacturing lead was quickly surpassed by Bolton and later by Oldham, with Manchester remaining the principal financial and distribution centre.

Before spinning, weaving and finishing the cloth, the cotton fibres have to be cleaned of seeds and dirt, initially by hand, in a process known as batting or scutching. However, by 1794 this was mechanised with Eli Whitney's invention of the cotton gin. Once cleaned, the fibres need to be combed out to ensure all remaining impurities are removed. Teasel heads provide the ideal means of doing this. The plant has a large, thistle-like head with many small hooks. The heads were fixed together to make a brush, which was then passed over the cotton, straightening and cleaning the fibres. This process is known as carding and produced long, thick lengths of cotton known as slivers. The fibres are then drawn out and lightly twisted together (roving) to make a thread suitable for spinning. During the mid-eighteenth century, John Mercer (1791–1866) discovered that soaking cotton thread with sodium hydroxide produced a stronger yarn that had a shiny or lustre finish, which took some dyes better than untreated cotton. This process became known as mercerisation.

The series of inventions that enabled the industry to be centralised in the mills gradually took away the livelihood of the handloom weavers. Once steam power could be applied to the factory machines, mills did not have to be near rivers and began to be built nearer towns. But the introduction of steam power was not without its critics. In 1801 one group of mill owners had to endure complaints that the engines were an 'offensive unsalutary nuisance', whereas Peel, Yates & Co., calico printers of Accrington, were praised in the *Blackburn Mail* newspaper for ensuring work could continue all year and with no stoppages for frost and drought. The industry seems to have had continual spells of plenty interspersed with slumps, which caused widespread deprivation. Downturns in the industry were the times when workers often moved to other jobs or other areas.

In 1826 there was a period of particular hardship and wages plummeted. This came to a head in April when, over a period of 3 days, a crowd of over 3,000 people smashed more than a 1,000 looms. Troops were called out. The mob headed for the Aitken & Lord factory at Chadderton, Lancashire, destroying the power looms there and stoning the soldiers. Finally the troops opened fire, killing four men and wounding many others.

Eventually the rioting died down, but fifty-three men and twelve women appeared at Lancaster Assizes in August 1826. Of this group, eight men and two women were transported for life and the rest imprisoned. Local newspapers carried the details of events, giving names of those involved and their eventual sentences.

The regular ups and downs of the trade were shadowed by protests as workers' wages were reduced, hours were curtailed or more machinery was introduced and workers became redundant.

In 1853 there was a major strike in Preston. Men were locked out from mills and Irish workers were brought over, many eventually sending for their families too. The strike lasted thirty-six weeks, but workers were gradually forced back to work. Records of these events may be found in newspapers of the day.

By mid-century over 5 million people were employed in the cotton industry. Prices were high and production soared. Added to this over-production, the Civil War in America (1861–1865) resulted in a cotton famine in Lancashire, because supplies of cotton from the southern states were disrupted by the North's economic blockade. Many businesses went bankrupt and unemployment spread. Lancashire had relied too heavily on one industry and when that failed, starvation was widespread. Towns throughout the country began sending money to help. Though some were too proud to accept it, thousands applied for relief, and this generated records, which are often found in local record offices. Calls for subscriptions and lists of those subscribing appeared in many newspapers. Records for these relief committees may be found at the local archives.

By the 1870s the industry was expanding once more, but other countries were beginning to produce cotton too and they were able and willing to invest in modern, faster machinery, such as the Northrop automatic power loom. Though cotton exports remained important, there was a gradual decline and now only about 7,000 people are employed in the textile industry in Lancashire. Not surprisingly, the majority of the archives in the north west have some records that relate to the textile industry.

Lancashire, though, was not the only area with a cotton industry. The Midlands was one of the first areas to produce cotton. Cromford Mill, built between 1772 and 1774, was Arkwright's first venture into full-scale factory production, using water power and bringing all workers together in one building. Partners included Jedediah Strutt and Peter Nightingale. Over the next hundred years the mills continued in production, but on a reduced scale. Masson Mills, built in about 1783 on the River Derwent at Matlock Bath, was further

Masson Mills, Matlock Bath, Derbyshire.

developed in the 1890s with new machinery to produce sewing thread. In 1897 it became part of the English Sewing Cotton Company, continuing in production until the end of the twentieth century. It is now a museum, where a range of machinery still produces small amounts of cloth for sale in the shop. Cromford Mill was not developed and was eventually sold, and has been used for a variety of business purposes.

Counties around Lancashire seem to have been more likely to build cotton mills than other textile factories. In 1781 a cotton mill opened at Ballasalla, Isle of Man, run initially by Abraham de la Pryme. He successfully produced cotton goods, employing a large number of Manx people, until in 1791 Liverpool customs decided to impose customs duties on the fabric. Despite pleas that the goods were not being 'imported' since the Isle of Man was part of Britain, the duty was imposed and Pryme took his business back to Lancashire.

Flintshire in Wales, particularly the Greenfield Valley, had a number of cotton mills. In 1777 John Smalley, who had previously been in partnership with Richard Arkwright in Nottingham, formed a new partnership with John Douglas and opened a cotton mill in Holywell. The business, which eventually became known as the Holywell Cotton Twist Co., took in apprentices from all over England, many from London but also from Lancashire, where both Smalley and Douglas continued to have business interests. Many of the shareholders of the business were also Lancashire businessmen. The Holywell Company failed in 1840–1842 and notices relating to this appear in the *London Gazette*.

The Yorkshire Dales were early centres of cotton working. An entry in Kirkby Malham baptism register on 4 December 1791 shows the baptism of Ann Robinson Spidit, daughter of Richard Spidit, tormentor of cotton wool – tormentor meant someone who beat the cotton to get rid of dirt and open up the bolls of cotton.

By 1835 the Craven district had over forty-four cotton mills, principally around Skipton, Barnoldswick and Settle. As late as 1851 the census shows that the cotton industry was still a large employer in the area with many workers coming from the neighbouring counties of Cumberland, Westmoreland and Lancashire, as well as all parts of Yorkshire, attracted by the higher wages.

In 1780 Clayton & Walshman opened Low Mill in Keighley to produce cotton using the new machinery patented by Richard Arkwright. A number of their apprentices, many of whom were pauper

Gibson Mill, Hebden Bridge.

apprentices from London, were sent down to Cromford in Derbyshire for training. Later they opened a second mill in Langcliffe, transporting some employees there from Keighley. In about the mid-nineteenth century Langcliffe mill was sold and converted to worsted. Halifax, Brighouse and Hebden Bridge had a large number of cotton mills at this time. Lord Holme Mill, generally known as Gibson Mill at Hebden Bridge, was a cotton mill built in 1800 but is now owned by the National Trust. Hebden Bridge became the centre of a major dispute when in July 1906 the fustian weavers went on strike to gain the same wage as their counterparts in Bury. The strikers held out for eighteen months, with good reports of the dispute in the local newspapers.

Though the East Riding is not normally associated with textiles, trade directories show that some mills were set up in and around Hull. The Kingston Cotton Mill Co. Ltd had large works in Cumberland Street and there is a list of shareholders in East Riding Archives. In 1838 Hull Flax and Cotton Mill Company employed about 200 people, with many of the operatives coming from Lancashire. However, the company failed in 1858 with large debts but somehow struggled on for another six years, although many workers drifted west to other mills. Some correspondence regarding liquidation is in East Riding Archives.

Even in the south of the country, occasionally cotton mills thrived. The Great Western Cotton Factory was set up in the 1830s in Bristol and continued until about 1925. Records from 1837–1877 can be found in the Bristol Record Office and include various deeds, trusts and correspondence, account book, cash book, letter book, samples book, miscellaneous papers and historical notes. Surprisingly, there was also a small cotton industry centred on Rickmansworth, Hertfordshire. Batchworth Mill was a water mill, which was originally used for cotton but by 1820 had been converted to process rags for paper.

During the twentieth century, firms frequently merged to form larger enterprises, which could take advantage of economies of scale. The two most successful businesses became Courtaulds and Coat Patons, both of which bought out many firms throughout the country. While the strategy appeared to be effective at first, by the 1960s, workforces were being cut. Gradually, companies and divisions were sold off as the area was hit by the general downturn in the textile industry during the 1970s.

The multitude of takeovers and mergers can make tracing records very difficult. An example of this can be seen in following the fortunes of two Derbyshire firms.

Cotton thread produced by J & P Coats and other companies.

The Evans family bought a number of industrial buildings at Darley Abbey, developing a cotton mill on the site in about 1780 and eventually employing over 600 people. Walter Evans & Co. produced cotton thread under the brand name 'Boar's Head' and had outlets all over the Midlands and London, becoming a limited company in 1905. The company was taken over by John Peacock, until in 1943 it became part of J & P Coats, which in turn transformed into Coats plc.

In the 1760s Jedediah Strutt built his first mill at Derby in partnership with William Woollat, expanding the partnership to include Samuel Need and developing a complex of mills over the next few years in Derby and Nottingham. Strutt also built his own mill in Belper. When the mill in Belper burnt down, Strutt's son designed and built the first 'fire-proof' mill, using brick and iron rather than wood for the interior. Strutt's descendants, trading as W & G Strutt, merged in 1893 with a number of other companies to form the English Sewing Cotton Company. In the 1960s the company took over Tootal Broadhurst Lee & Co., and merged with the Calico Printers Association Ltd to become English Calico Limited. This name, too, eventually changed to the Tootal Group, which was taken over by Coats Viyella in the 1990s and is now part of Coats plc.

Some of the records for Walter Evans & Co. are at the Derbyshire Record Office; some are in Glasgow University, as part of the J & P Coats collection there. Archives relating to Strutt's and the English Sewing Cotton Company are with Derbyshire Record Office, but some are also in the Archives and Local Studies at Manchester Central Library; family papers of Barons Belper (Strutt family) are with Nottinghamshire Archives; records of Tootal Broadhurst Lee are in Bolton Archives, while those of the Calico Printers Association are at the Colour Museum, Bradford. These relate to just a few of the companies that became part of the Coats Group. Other archives also hold some papers that may relate to these firms as part of correspondences etc. with other businesses.

Useful websites include:

- ww.spartacus.schoolnet.co.uk/IndustrialRevolution.htm.
- www.spinningtheweb.org.uk.
- www.cottontown.org/page.cfm?pageid=257.

5.1 Calico printing

Calico is a type of cotton cloth, which, after bleaching, washing and drying, can be printed with intricate patterns. When the Huguenots fled the continent in the 1680s, they brought their skills of calico printing to England, settling particularly around London. Calico began to be imported by the East India Company, but in 1699 there were riots in protest and during the early eighteenth century its production was banned, as it was too much in competition with the existing silk and wool industry. The calico producers solved this problem by making fustian instead – a mixture of linen and cotton, which was quite legal. It was not until almost the end of the century that the ban was lifted and pure cotton calico was again made.

An extensive textile industry thrived in the Lea Valley, partly because of the nearness of a good water supply. By the seventeenth century calico printing and dye works were established here and in nearby Lambeth, Poplar, Richmond and Wapping.

The Wandle Valley in Surrey, too, provided a plentiful supply of water for power and industry use. Many mills, including about twenty calico printing works, were built here; the nearness to London ensured both a workforce and a market. Mitcham became a centre for bleaching of calico for London, quickly establishing itself as a central market for the area.

Merton Abbey is well known through its association with William Morris and Liberty but actually opened as a calico printing works sometime in the early eighteenth century. Using bankruptcy notices it is possible to trace businesses in the factory. These include a partnership between James Newton, John Rivers, John Leach and Richard Howard, which ended in about 1786. Fenning, Halfhide and Co. was run as a partnership between William Fenning, James Halfhide the Elder, James Halfhide the Younger and Edward Halfhide, who left in about 1788, but seem to have shared the premises with Benjamin Vaughan, who also became bankrupt at about the same time. John Leach then went into partnership with Thomas Bennett, Thomas Bartlett and William Keatch, but this partnership ended in 1801. James Newton, James Collin and James Anderson were partners in the building until about 1806, while John Leach and Thomas Bennett rearranged their partnership, taking in Thomas Bartlett and Isaac Hellier, which lasted until 1809. The Littler family seem to have been there longest, starting as a partnership between three brothers – William Littler, Edmund Littler and Charles Littler, but William and Charles left this partnership in 1836 and Edmund continued on his own. Their mother, Mary Ann Littler, also had a hand in the business, though it is not clear whether it was a separate business of her own or in partnership with her sons. However, in 1863 Edmund, William and another son, James, and her widowed daughter, Sarah Witham, acted as guarantors for their mother when she was declared bankrupt. William, Edmund and James formed a partnership to run the business until 1868 when James left. The Littler business continued, eventually making prints for Liberty & Co. before the factory was bought out by Liberty itself. Liberty ended their production in 1972 but other firms (Vita-Tex Ltd, Riseline Ltd and Merton Fabrics Ltd) continued until 1982. The records for Liberty & Co. are at City of Westminster Archives Centre. Also, there are a number of photographs, including some of members of the Littler family. Some pattern books of William Fenning & Co. survive – contact The National Archives for details of access.

By the mid-eighteenth century much of the calico printing had moved northwards, particularly to Lancashire. In 1890 nearly fifty firms amalgamated to form the Calico Printers Association Ltd, with its head office in Manchester and print works throughout the country. Some of the records for this company are at Manchester Archives and Local Studies, while some others are at the Modern Records Centre, University of Warwick as part of the British Clothing Industry Association archive. After the First World War, the calico industry declined along with the rest of the textile industry.

Derbyshire had a thriving calico-printing industry, particularly in the Sett Valley, along with cotton and woollen mills and dye works. New Mills included a number of cotton mills, which continued the finishing industry (bleaching, dyeing, printing or adding other finishes to cloth) into the twentieth century, though many mills were demolished in 1960s.

Chapter 6

THE LINEN INDUSTRY

Linen is produced from the flax plant, which is difficult to grow and must be harvested at just the right time and in the correct way to create the best linen. The plant then has to go through many processes to create a yarn that can be woven.

Rippling involves passing the plant fibres over coarse combs to remove seeds, leaves and dirt. The seeds can be used for oil. The plant is then soaked in water or chemicals to separate and rot away the woody bark, which is found around the flax fibres. This is known as

Hemp and flax claims, Doncaster newspaper, 1791.

retting. The stems are next rolled to crush any remaining bark and then rinsed in clean water. After drying, the process known as breaking and scutching or swingling takes place. The flax is rolled again to break up the stalks, then passed through a scutching machine to separate out the bast fibres which will be used to make linen, from the bits of bark or shives. This was once a hand process, done by beating the flax with bats.

Hackling or heckling involves combing to separate the long fibres (line) from the short fibres (tow). The line fibres are spun into a fine yarn, while the tow fibres are first carded and then spun into a heavier, coarser yarn.

Once these processes are completed the yarn can be woven on its own or used with other fibres to produce cloth, which then needs finishing before use.

Cloth may be laundered and finished by mangling or beetling. Mangling tools include wooden rolling pins or glass 'rubbers', which exert pressure on the surface of the wet cloth lying on a hard surface. In other places the fabric was beaten with mallets. This processing breaks up the surface fibres and smoothes them so the fabric takes on a sheen.

Flax was found in many areas, though much was imported from Ireland through Liverpool and Chester, or from the Baltic ports of Riga, Narva and St Petersburg, shipping into Newcastle and Hull and thence by road inland. During the Napoleonic Wars the Baltic ports were closed, and thus new links were established with Ireland, where eventually the linen industry came to be of prime importance. Finished goods were sent down to London or exported directly from western ports to Virginia or the West Indies.

Some of the earliest references to flax relate to monasteries. Whalley Abbey, near Clitheroe, is known to have received a small amount of its tithes in flax and linen. Norfolk, particularly Norwich, was an important centre for the linen industry, though this had declined considerably by the fourteenth century.

Initially the industry was 'subsistence' level, i.e., sufficient spun for home use, often for sacking or rough outer garments. However, spinning was also organised on a 'putting out' system, particularly around Garstang, Furness, Lancaster, Darlington, Stockport and Norwich, where coastal transport was available, but also in inland areas such as Wigton and Penrith near the main road south. Much of the finished cloth was sold locally or at fairs like Appleby and Roseley. Towards the end of the sixteenth century, emigrants from Flanders arrived in England, settling in the south. The Flemish developed and improved the existing cloth production and introduced thread twisting – making linen thread from locally grown flax. Some thread continued to be made in Kent into the nineteenth century, and was used locally for ropes or hop bags. Some of the immigrants moved north, bringing with them improved cloth-making skills, particularly in relation to flax.

In 1787 John Kendrew and Thomas Porterhouse of Darlington, backed by many of the local manufacturers, developed a machine that would successfully spin flax. This was the breakthrough that was needed to enable the development of a factory system. Manufacturers began to appear in trade directories of the time. William Richardson had a 'lint'-spinning manufactory at Ouseburn, later to be joined in the town by Clark, Plummer & Co. By 1827/8 John Hodgson, D & J Livingston and James Scott (at Gateshead) had established linen manufactories at Newcastle. John Lodge, Jasper Whitfield & Son were in Stockton, while Geo & Thomas Ellerson, Messrs Ianson, Toulmin & Ord, Francis Kipling & Son, Francis Robinson and William Thompson were operating in Darlington. As is often the case, supporting

Catherine Street Mill, Whitehaven.

industries also sprang up. George Rutherford in Bath Lane, Newcastle, made the heckles needed as part of the process of preparing the flax for subsequent spinning.

In the late eighteenth century a bounty was paid for flax and hemp grown. Claims for this bounty can sometimes be found in local archives and lists often appeared in local newspapers.

In its heyday, to about 1840, flax-spinning mills in the north-east area employed almost 6,500 people. In Darlington, the Kipling family had been weavers of linen cloth but started weaving carpets in about 1813. As the linen industry declined, more and more production was switched to carpets.

After the invention of spinning machinery, mills began to be built resulting in the industry moving away from the traditional areas and into the valleys – for example, around the Lake District, where there was water for power and access to ports such as Whitehaven – and goods began to be sold in shops in the towns. The north west seems to have specialised in the production of coarse linen, sailcloth and canvas rather than compete with the cotton industry. This strategy worked well at first, but then shipping turned to steam power, the demand for canvas reduced and resulted in a decline in the linen industry in the area.

Some of the earliest factories were built by Quakers, particularly in the north west. John Kendrew of Darlington, who invented the first flax-spinning machine, belonged to the Friends, as did Jonathan and William Harris, who built Derwent Mills at Cockermouth in 1834, and Charles Parker, who ran High Mills at Bentham in 1785. This continued as a linen mill until the 1860s, when production moved to silk. In 1809 Joseph Bell built Catherine Street Mill in Whitehaven, which continued in production until 1853 and has now been converted into flats. The mills ousted the small cottage industry but were, in turn, themselves pushed out during the nineteenth century, by the move to cotton production centred around Manchester or woollen production in the West Riding of Yorkshire.

Linen production in Yorkshire was focused in the north initially, particularly around Knaresborough, Northallerton and Ripon during the late eighteenth and early nineteenth centuries. In 1828 the dyeing industry centred on Osmotherley and Yarm, while Northallerton had nine linen factories around the town but by 1893 these were reduced to two – William and John Pattison and John Wilford and Sons, both of Brompton. Links were soon established with Barnsley and Darlington, with many workers migrating to and from the town-based linen industry. A number of flax mills were built or converted from fulling mills and some pauper apprentices were sent from North Yorkshire villages into these linen mills.

Employment in North Yorkshire changed – in 1851 Osmotherley had 54 employed in linen working, while Brompton had 175 linen workers. By 1891 this had fallen to 26 and 125 respectively. Workers either changed jobs or moved away, often to the west of the county where other textile jobs were available or up to the coalfields of Middlesbrough and Newcastle.

A few mills were built around Sheffield, Conisborough, Easingwold, Stocksbridge and Ecclesfield. Flax was grown around the Isle of Axholme. In later times, Barnsley and Leeds became the two main centres of linen production in Yorkshire.

William Wilson is credited with founding the Barnsley linen industry, beginning in about 1744 by employing mainly handloom weavers in their own cottages. About a hundred years later, the power loom was in use in a factory built by Thomas Taylor. Barnsley Record Office has photographs of this mill, together with oral histories from previous workers. Numerous deeds, leases and mortgages in both Barnsley and Sheffield Record Offices refer to linen manufacturers of Barnsley.

The building of linen factories brought workers in not only from the surrounding area, but also from Ireland from the mid-eighteenth century onwards. By 1914 the industry was in severe decline, faced

Thomas Taylor's mill, Barnsley Ordnance Survey map, 1893.

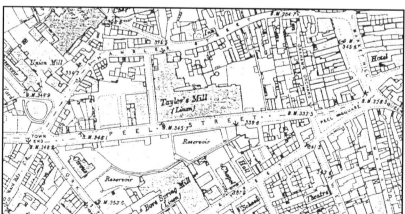

with competition from Scotland but primarily from the Irish linen industry itself.

In 1788 John Marshall took up the linen machinery invented by John Kendrew and Thomas Porthouse from Darlington, improved it and built up his business to become one of the foremost producers of linen in England, initially in Scotland Mill before building the magnificent Temple Mills at Holbeck. The firm continued in existence until 1886 when poor trading forced it to close. Some records are in the Brotherton Library, Special Collections but none refer specifically to workers at the factory.

Linen was used in diverse ways. Lighter yarns could be made into towels, covers and drill, while the very finest was woven into cambric and lawn. Heavier fabrics, including sailcloth, canvas, tarpaulin and sacking, were all used extensively in the shipping industry and hence tended to be made near ports. Even small ports boasted some factories. Whitby's linen industry manufactured sailcloth, ropes and sackcloth, but few records remain, apart from occasional apprenticeship indentures, such as that of John Walker to Thomas Chilton, sail maker of Whitby (a photocopy of which is at the Whitby Literary and Philosophical Society), and evidence of trade directories and census returns.

Other areas in which flax was used include Fordingbridge, in Hampshire, which had a considerable flax industry, producing large amounts of ticking, used for covering mattresses. By the end of the eighteenth century almost 500 were employed in this industry but 50 years later it had declined in the face of northern competition.

One of the earliest types of industry in Hounslow was a flax mill, owned by Messrs Jones & Shewell, which took a number of pauper apprentices from the city of London. London Metropolitan Archives has a Deed of Covenant from 1821 relating to this, which includes a schedule with the names of all the apprentices, the age at which they were apprenticed and where they came from.

Stephens Brothers and Martin Ltd, which closed in the 1970s, originated in the flax business of Stephens Brothers from Bridport, Dorset. George Martin later joined the firm and together they formed a limited company. In 1942 St Philip's Mills were leased to J Bryant Ltd, which eventually bought out the company. Records for Stephen Brothers & Martin include, 1851–1961: private ledger, wages book, accident book, correspondence, deeds, plans, valuations and inventories and photographs. For Joseph Bryant, 1747–1974: private ledgers, ledgers, journal, invoice book, apprenticeship indentures, deeds and family wills.

In searching for ancestors in this branch of textiles it is important to remember that for most people it was simply a secondary occupation and therefore often does not appear in trade directories or other records. Sometimes the only reference is found in a will, when a stock of linen yarn will be noted. Flax dressers, who prepared the yarn in its initial stages, were often dealers as well. Since the process generally took place in a town workshop, that is where they tended to live, while spinning was a rural, cottage industry until late in the eighteenth century and therefore tended to be done by poorer members of society. Flax, however, takes longer to prepare, so many small dealers in flax took to producing the yarn themselves, putting out the weaving to others or buying cloth from other small clothiers and these dealers may appear in trade directories.

The linen industry enjoyed a number of revivals. During the American Civil War, the decline in cotton supplies encouraged the growing of flax in the Norfolk and Cambridgeshire fens as a substitute, though this lasted only until normal supplies of cotton were resumed. In 1883 there was a revival of the linen industry as part of the 'Arts and Crafts Movement', inspired by John Ruskin and others who opposed industrialisation. Around Langdale a small group supplied flax to poor people who then spun and wove cloth to provide themselves with a small income. During the First World War, as had happened during the American Civil War, cotton was in short supply and flax was again grown to supply the linen industry in order to make canvas for the troops. Flax companies continued for only a few years after the war. In the 1930s King George V took an interest, producing flax on the Sandringham Estate and supporting the setting up of a flax mill in West Newton, Norfolk. The business continued throughout the war but costs rose and it became uneconomic to continue. In 1958 the machinery was sold off and the factory closed.

Chapter 7

LACE MAKING

Lace fabric is lightweight, patterned and with open holes in the work, which may be made by machine or by hand. Originally lace was made with linen yarn and later with cotton yarn, which gives a finer quality. Cotton is also more elastic, breaks less often and is not as expensive.

Removing threads in a specific pattern from cloth already woven produces drawn thread work, but more often lace is made up from the interweaving of a single thread in such a way as to create open spaces as part of the fabric.

Cut work is a technique in which parts of the cloth are cut away leaving a hole that is filled or reinforced with lace or embroidery. Lace can also be crocheted or knitted.

Needle lace is made using a needle and thread. Knotted lace includes macramé and tatting, which is made with a shuttle or a tatting needle

Bobbin lace is made on a firm pillow rested on the knee. A pricked-out pattern is tacked to the pillow and the thread is weighted by bobbins, made in a variety of different shapes and weights. The thread, which is held in place with pins, is woven together by turning the bobbins. Early bobbins and pins were made from bone, so this process is also known as bone lace. Pillow lace is another name for this technique.

Initially the lace, when finished, had a rough surface, which was traditionally burnt off by pulling the cloth over red hot cylinders fast enough not to damage the fabric. Later a process called gassing was invented, which used gas flames that could be applied to either the cloth or thread and speeded up the whole process. The lace also had to be bleached, then dipped in a starch mixture and squeezed through rollers to extract the excess liquid before finally being put onto frames in a stretching room to dry out. The pieces had to be stretched carefully and rubbed over with flannel to even out the starch. Sometimes fans would be used to speed up the drying.

Lace making was certainly found in eastern England before the seventeenth century, for example, in Amersham, barely 30 miles from London, where workers specialised in making black lace. However, lace making tended to be a cottage industry, carried on alongside other occupations. The lace was made into a long strip that could then be sold to a dealer. Lace dealers provided the designs and purchased yardage from the lace makers. Towcester and Buckingham became early centres of fine lace. Later lace schools were opened to train children in the art, but these had largely died out by 1880s.

Parts of Buckinghamshire, particularly over the Chilterns, have very poor soil, making farming rather unproductive. This led to the need for a second income and many turned to lace making to supplement, or even provide, an income. Lace schools developed at High Wycombe, Marlow (established 1626) and Stony Stratford. Olney, too, had its lace school, the finished product being known as 'Bucks Point'.

In Bedford, the Lester family were the most prominent lace merchants, dealing with lace makers for many miles around the city. However, as dealers, they had no employees in the formal sense, so no records remain of the hundreds of ordinary men and women who made up their beautiful designs. Bedfordshire and Northamptonshire lace is very different from Devonshire lace, which developed during the nineteenth century as a result of changes in fashion and machinery. Gradually, the lace industry dwindled and considerable poverty was caused by its demise. New machinery could produce the lace more quickly and of a reasonable quality.

The Midlands Lace Association was formed in 1891 to help the industry, encouraging people to buy locally made lace and providing training. North Bucks Lace Association was formed in 1897 and the Buckinghamshire Cottage Workers' Agency in 1906, the latter being set up by Harry Armstrong, selling lace via a catalogue and eventually employing hundreds of part-time workers. Later he built a lace factory at Olney, where the pieces of lace were stitched together. This has now been converted to flats. While these associations are frequently mentioned in local history books, there appears to be no remaining records of employees.

John Heathcoat was one of the first to develop a machine that could make bobbin lace, setting up his factory in Loughborough in about 1809. However, workers who feared for their jobs attacked the lace factory in 1816 and, as a result of this, Heathcote moved his factory to Devon. Many of his workers from Leicester moved with him to the

West Country. When Queen Victoria married in 1840 she used Honiton lace for her veil. Then, as now, the royal 'seal of approval' gave a huge boost to the Devon industry. The firm continued for over 150 years, diversifying into other fabrics and opening a factory in Cornwall in the 1940s, making elastic fabrics. Records for this firm are now at the Devon Record Office and include plans, financial and production records, correspondence and family papers, 1816–1970. Log books, pattern books, pension-fund register and various staff papers dating from 1898 to 1970 are at the Tiverton Museum.

A different machine, making fine lace, was invented in 1813 by John Leavers from Nottingham. It was modified in 1853 by Samuel Fergusson to make more patterned lace. This was used extensively around Nottingham and Long Eaton, where factories employed hundreds of workers until the industry's decline in the early twentieth century. It was forbidden to export the machines, but three enterprising men from Nottingham (Robert Webster, Richard Bonington and Samuel Clark) smuggled machinery out to Calais and founded a highly successful lace industry there. Many English folk migrated to the town to find work and settled there.

The Isle of Wight also had a lace-making factory, established at Broadlands, near Newport, in 1826 by John Nunn, who came from the Midlands. This eventually employed almost 800 people, mainly women, from the local area, both in the factory and as outworkers in their cottages. Nunn's descendant, Henry William Nunn, continued trading but the business closed in 1868. The local archives have a detailed article about the history of the firm and its owning family, but no other specific records.

Chapter 8

THE SILK INDUSTRY

Silk comes from the cocoon of the silkworm. The cocoons are collected and the pupae killed by heating the cocoons. The cocoons need to be sorted according to quality. The best quality is used to produce warp threads, which need to be stronger than the weft threads. The outside and inside silk of the cocoon is of poorer quality, called frison or reeling waste, while the middle silk is the finest quality. The cocoons are put into warm water to soften the gum that holds the cocoon together and the long, continuous thread is carefully 'reeled' off. Several cocoons are unwound together, because the individual filaments are too fine. The sericin or gum remaining on the silk binds these strands into one. The silk strands or filaments, which can be as much as a mile long, are then put on to large reels known as swifts.

The middle, fine-quality silk is twisted together to produce a thread strong enough for use and the process is called throwing rather than spinning. Throwing involves the revolving of two sets of bobbins at different speeds. The frison or waste can be cut into lengths, which can be combed into noils and used in woollen blends of cloth, or spun into yarns that are used for weft, embroidery and ribbon silk.

Silk absorbs dye better than any other product and can produce some stunning results. New materials, too, were eventually produced. At the end of the nineteenth century a British invention of artificial silk became known as viscose rayon, manufactured extensively from 1910 onwards (see Chapter 10).

Though Wandsworth had its share of Flemish and French textile workers who established silk weaving, calico printing, dyeing and bleaching in the area, Spitalfields, originally part of Stepney until it became an independent parish in 1729, is probably the most well-known silk area. It was here that many of the French and Flemish weavers settled in the sixteenth century, and again in large numbers in the seventeenth century, and began their silk-producing industry, soon rivalling the quality of cloth produced in France. The original French families sometimes anglicised their names, such as changing Le Noir to Black. By the eighteenth century these families had become the masters and manufacturers, while much of the work was done in the home so the silk workers themselves, who were often English or Irish who had come and settled in this part of London, were relatively poor. Disputes frequently developed between the workers and employers, or between Huguenot/English workers and Irish workers, leading to many riots. In 1773 the Spitalfields Weavers Act was passed which ensured that wages were set by magistrates, the amount being binding on both employer and employee. However, generally both sides negotiated a settlement and then went to the magistrate to ratify it, the result being that the agreement was recorded, with the names of each of the journeymen who petitioned the magistrates at the end of each document. Some of these records survived and are to be found in London Metropolitan Archives.

The Act did not help the silk weavers as they expected. The silk throwster's job was not highly skilled and could easily be done on water-powered machinery in factories away from the city. Because the wages were regulated, many businesses began to move away from London into the surrounding counties, leaving the Spitalfields workers in even worse poverty. When the Spitalfields Act was repealed in 1824 wages fell even further and many workers may have migrated elsewhere or changed occupation at this time.

In 1812 the firm of Swaislands had established a factory at Crayford in Kent which continued until the firm's dissolution in 1866 (records in BT31 at The National Archives). Some of the designs and patterns books have survived in the Victoria & Albert Museum and Maidstone Museum, respectively. David Evans & Co., silk printers, moved from Spitalfields to Crayford using the River Cray for water power. Later, Evans took over the silk-printing works that had been established in Crayford by Augustus Applegath (1788–1871). Applegath was a prolific inventor and engineer, and many of his patent records are in The National Archives, while others, together with some leases and agreements, are at the Bexley Local Studies Centre. The business continued for over 150 years but in 1989 formed, with Vanners Ltd, a new company known as Silk Industries. The company closed its Crayford works in 2001 and moved the remaining business to Macclesfield. Many artefacts were passed on to the Bexley Museum, including casting blocks, fabric samples, pattern books and silk screens. Other documents – order books, administrative forms, advertising scrap books, silk samples, financial papers and a number of building plans – are at Bexley Local Studies Centre and some (minutes, register of members, financial and wages records and order books, etc.) are at The National Archives.

Applegath moved his original silk works to Dartford in the 1840s where the business became known as the Dartford Printing Works, owned successively by John Hyland & Co. and then Warner & Sons. The business closed just before the Second World War and plans of the buildings can be seen in the Centre for Kentish Studies, but the business records do not appear to have been deposited.

The Victorians seem to have been obsessed with death, which is not surprising considering the high death rate from cholera and other diseases. They required large numbers of mourning clothes. In 1809 Grout & Baylis built their crape mill at Ponders End, London. The company produced black crape and the factory soon expanded to employ over 200 people until its closure in 1894. Joseph and George Grout, with their partners, were major contributors to the industry's

The Courtauld Fountain, Braintree.

success, producing new types of fabric from 1822 onwards, including 'Norwich crape'. The brothers had substantial factories in Yarmouth and Norwich, as well as Suffolk, Essex, Middlesex, Manchester and Scotland. These were mostly closed in 1890 and work centred on Yarmouth before that too closed in 1974. Surviving records are principally in Norfolk Record Office and consist of various deeds of partnership, plans and minutes of meetings. Enfield Local History Unit has some papers and correspondence relating to the Ponders End mill. Fire-insurance records for the company can be found at the Guildhall.

Other large employers were Carter Vavasour & Rix of Cheapside, John Vanner & Sons, which later moved to Sudbury, Daniel Walters & Son, which produced furniture silks and damasks, and Warner & Sons, which opened New Mill in Braintree in 1895. Warner & Sons moved to Milton Keynes and closed the Braintree factory in 1971. The Warner Textile Archive has now been opened in Braintree, in the original New Mills, now renamed Warners Mill. This archive records the history of textile designs and manufacture with examples of woven and printed

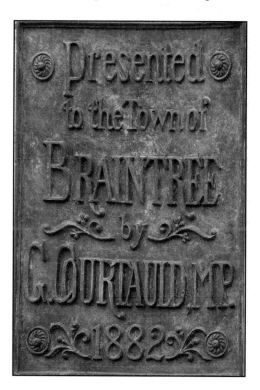

Plaque on the Courtauld
Fountain, Braintree.

fabric, together with a collection of information relating to the company and its former employees.

Essex became a major centre for silk when in 1809 George Courtauld opened a silk mill in Braintree, gradually expanding until he employed thousands of workers. He specialised in producing crape and even invented a more efficient spindle for the silk machines. Young apprentices from the London workhouses were often brought here or to the later factories of Samuel Courtauld in Halstead and Bocking. The firm of Courtauld, Taylor & Courtauld expanded until by the mid-nineteenth century they employed about 2,000 people. The business continued to grow and eventually became a massive conglomerate, but also supported local people by subscribing to schools, hospitals, town halls and parks.

Coggeshall began as an agricultural market town and then enjoyed a brief spell as a centre for the wool industry but went on to became famous for lace and silk. Almost 1,000 people were employed in John Hall's silk mill by 1860, but financial difficulties led him to transfer the business to Stephen Brown in 1865. By 1877 the mill had closed completely. Silk mills were to be found at Tring, where N M Rothschild & Sons owned a mill in Brook Street, employing about 600 people and managed by John Akers. Sale particulars of this (1872) are in the Centre for Buckinghamshire Studies. T R Shute established a business at Rookery Silk Mills, Watford, and further silk mills were at Baldock, Hitchin, Hatfield and Rickmansworth. The site of Charles Woollam's silk mill at Redbourn and the house built for its manager are part of the Redbourn Museum.

In 1824 a silk throwing mill was set up at Glemsford, near Sudbury, Suffolk, eventually adding a dye works. In its heyday it employed over 200 and by 1830 silk was being made in Haverhill, Suffolk. Stephen Walters of Spitalfields built the first factory, Kemp and Sons adding a second mill in about 1858 with a third by J Vanner & Sons in 1873. Walters took over the firm of Kipling and Co. and production continued until the 1880s.

Whitchurch Mill, Hampshire, was a fulling mill bought by William Maddick in 1816. Maddick was a wealthy silk merchant and haberdasher with property in Love Lane, Aldermanbury, London, for which there is a fire-insurance certificate at the Guildhall Library, and was in partnership with Samuel Calvert as lace merchant and silk manufacturer. Maddick converted Whitchurch Mill to produce silk. By 1838 it had changed hands but was still producing silk and employing

TRADES' DIRECTORY. 1371

SHOPKEEPERS—continued.
Woods W. 31 New York st. Brighton
Woodward Mrs. M. 40 Trafalgar street, Brighton
Woodward H. Fallbridge, East Grinstead
Woodyard J. Richard street, Chatham
Woolard T. Haverhill
Woolley Mrs. A. High street, Watford
Worley P. Turnham green
Worsfold G. Rudgewick
Worskett W. Hockley, Rayleigh
Worsley J. Tilehouse street, Hitchin
Worsley N. Yalding, Maidstone
Wratten Mrs. M.A. Bear's isle, Tenterdn
Wren H. Fallbridge, East Grinstead
Wright B. Higham, Rochester
Wright Mrs. E. Charlwood, Crawley
Wright G. Merton
Wright H. Roxwell, Chelmsford
Wright J. Billericay
Wright J. Church street, Rickmansworth
Wright J. Horley, Crawley
Wright J. Littlebury, Saffron Walden
Wright J. Peldon, Colchester
Wright J. Buntingford
Wright Mrs. M. Kensal gn. Harrow rd
Wright R. 5 Waterloo place, Lewes
Wright S. M. Ashdon, Linton
Wright Mrs. S. Crowley's wharf, East Greenwich
Wright W. High street, Maldon
Wyatt J. Batchworth, Rickmansworth
Wybrew J. Wareside, Ware
Wybrow W. Springfield bl. Chelmsford
Wyles T. Lower Rainham, Sittingbourne
Wyles W. Upchurch, Sittingbourne
Yelding B. High street, Godalming
Yeomans Mrs. M. Charles st. Woolwich
Yielding G. Bohemia terrace, Hastings
Yonwin C. 25 Star street, Gravesend
Young C. Starch green, Hammersmith
Young F. Horley, Crawley
Young G. Water end, Gt. Gaddesden
Young J. Back street, Hitchin
Young J. Clay street, Walthamstow
Young J. Wood end,Ardeley,Buntingfrd
Young T. Pawkham, Dartford

SILK & VELVET MANUFAC-TURERS.
Brooks T. East street, Coggeshall
Campbell, Harrison & Lloyd (J. Castle, manager), Military road, Colchester
Carter, Vavasseur & Rix (G. Vavasseur, agent), Bocking end, Braintree
Coatzuald S. & Co. Halstead mills, Hlstd
Evans D. Tring
Glaskin J. 4 Retreat place, Homerton
Goodson & Son, Lit. Coggeshall, Kelvdn
Hall J. & Son, West street, Coggeshall, & at Maldon & Tiptree
Henderson, Arundel & Henderson (G. Shead, agent), High st. Braintree
Parker J. Silk mill, Tring
Roberts R. Haverhill
Sanderson & Reid (J. Wheeler, agent), High street, Braintree
Vanner & Sons (E. Spearman, agent), Pound end, Braintree
Walters D. & Son (T. C. Cheeseman, agent), Pound end, Braintree
Westmacott T. Church street, Coggeshall, & 8 Noble street, London
Willson, Casey & Co. Ballington, Sdbry
Wilson B. West street, Coggeshall, at 37 Wallbrook, London

SILK MERCERS.
Acworth & Hughes,High st.Chelmsford
Adams, Benness & Son, East st.Chelstr
Alger William, 2, 3 & 4 St. James's st. Brighton
Allen H. South street, Chichester
Aris W. 8 High street, Croydon
Barrow E. High street, Ramsgate
Beard S. High street, Saffron Walden
Blake J. Walton-on-Thames, Esher
Bourne H. High street, Ramsgate
Braund George, High street, Dartford
Bryant J. & W. Week street, Maidstone
Carter J. George street, Richmond
Cocks Robert & Co. Fore st. Hertford

Collier W. Bexley heath
Cooper R. High street, Bognor
Corke I. Serenoaks
Cove H. High road, Tottenham
Easter F. Town, Enfield
Edwards C. Parade, Tunbridge Wells
Elliott R. Parade, Tunbridge Wells
Ellis Alfred, 1 Harbour street, Ramsgate
Ellis T. High street, Tunbridge Wells
Flicker E. High street, Reigate
Gadd H. 9 & 10 South street, Chichester
Gask Henry, 5 & 6 Wellington place, Hastings
Good J. High street, Watford
Goodman & Co. High street, Uxbridge
Gosling & Susans, Broad st. Folkestone
Griffin & Son, 19 Head street, Colchestr
Grist & Kenward, 63 Queen st. Ramsgte
Hall J. Clarence street, Kingston
Hannington (Smith) & Sons, 2, 3 & 4 North street, Brighton
Haseldine J. 193 Snargate st. Dover
Hellen Thomas, 140 High st. Margate
Highgason W. J. 25 Spital st.Guildford
Hogben G. Mile town, Sheerness
James G. E. Lovefield street, Dartford
Jones W. High street, Upper Sydenham
Kenward T. Stone street, Cranbrook
Killick & Back, Market place, Dover
Kirkby J. T. Fore st. Up. Edmonton
Leigh & Pilcher, 180 Snargate st. Dover
Levett Walter, Queen street, Arundel
Loader J. 36 East street, Chichester
Longley & Co. Parade, Tunbridge Wells
Lyon William, Sittingbourne
Metcalf W. & F. Bench street, Dover
Mills H. G. & Co. High st. Tunbridge
Murton G. Market place, Faversham
Nash & Lukey, High street, Bromley
Noakes W. High st. Tunbridge Wells
Palmer C. & J. Sevenoaks
Palmer P. High street, Highgate
Pocock G. 22 King's road, Brighton
Rickards W.& Co. the Village, Lewisham
Salmon John, 50 High street, Colchester
Sayer J. & A. 50 North street, Brighton
Seaton & Son, High street, Richmond
haw John, Albion house, High street, Ramsgate
Shewell M. Market st. Saffron Walden
Sibley R. G. 75 Western road, Brighton
Skinner George & Richard, Victoria house, Gabriel's hill, Maidstone
Smith J. A. High street, Watford
Syrett H. 23 Harbour street, Ramsgate
Tanner J. Parade, Tunbridge Wells
Tapply E. L. 24 High st. Ramsgate
Thompson E.High road, Low.Tottenham
Vickridge F. J. & W. H. High street, Uxbridge
Weale J. High street, Godalming
Westwood T. E. High street, Reigate
Whibley A. Sittingbourne

SILK PRINTERS.
Downing J. Mitcham common
Evans D. & Co. Crayford, Dartford
Littler Mrs. M. a. Merton
Swaisland C. Crayford, Dartford
Tucker J. West Ham Abbey,WestHam
Welch & Margetson, Phipps bridge, Mitcham

SILK THROWSTERS.
Arnold R. Silk mills, Lewisham lane
Brown S. Dend lane, Colchester
Hall J. & Son, West street, Coggeshall, & at Union street, Maldon, & Inworth, Kelvedon
Lawton J. Rickmansworth silk mills
Rodrick E., L. & B. Pebmarsh, Colchester, & Old Broad street, London
Shute T. R. Rookery silk mills, Watfrd
Woollam J. & Son, Abbey mill lane, St. Alban's

SILVERSMITHS.
Ainsworth J. B. 56 High st. Croydon
April J. Ballington, Sudbury
Ballard H. Stone street, Cranbrook
Barker J. East street, Chichester
Challen W. 65 King's road, Brighton
Cockburn J. R. King street, Richmond

Chambers W. D. 127 St. James's street, Brighton
Cogill H. W. 65 High street,Chatham
Cohen M. 160 Snargate street, Dover
Cragg E. N. 25 High street, Colchester
Davey E. L. & Sons, 195 High st.Lewes
De la Cour G. 327 & 59 High street, Chatham
Elliott & Son, High street, Ashford
Foikard D. M. 138 & 139 North street, Brighton
Glading F. 45 & 47 King's rd. Brighton
Greenwood W. 51 High st. Rochester
Hall K. 77 Snargate street, Dover
Hart M. 56 & 57 St. Peter's street, Canterbury, & 6 Tontine st.Folkestone
Hayward L. High street, Ashford
Itukins G. H. Tenterden
Joel J. 89 St. James's street, Brighton
Lazarus N. 16 Sun street, Canterbury
Lyons L. 17 New road, Brighton
Lyons S. 112 High street, Rochester
Marks E. Fore street, Brnintree
Marsh T. High street, Dorking
Marshall C.25 Blackheath hill,Grnwch
Martin E. 6 Bartholomews, Brighton
Martin J. Court street, Faversham
Mason C. 28 St. George's st.Canterbury
Masters J. Tenterden
Moor & Son, Royal Pelham arcade & 23 Robertson street, Hastings
Moses M. 29 Strand street, Dover
Oxbrow W. Bank street, Braintree
Pyke J. 202 High street, Chatham
Sherwood J. Market place, Faversham
Solomon S. 1 High street, Cliffe, Lewes
Stedman Mrs. C. S. High st.Godalming
Three-her T. S. King st. Hammersmith
Trizgs W. 120 High street, Guildford
Wilmshurst T. East street, Chichester
Wing Miss S. Grent square, Braintree

SLATE MERCHANTS.
Andrews T. East Mousley, Kingston
Austin & Lee, 12 Upper Bedford street & 16 Warwick grove, Brighton, & at Newhaven
Averst T. Strand, Rye
Biffin H. W. & Son, Eastgate,Chichester
Slaber William; office, 11 Manchester street, Marine parade; slate yards in Edward street & Henry street, Brighton
Boulcott Joseph & Co. Causeway, Bishop Stortford; Amwell end,Ware, & at Limehouse
Brown J. Heybridge, Maldon, & Chelmsford
Buckwell A. & C. D. Shoreham
Butt J. F. 30 Queen's road, Brighton
Edwards W. 1 Market street, & 30 & 31 Devonshire place, Brighton
Finnis Steriker, New bridge, Dover
Fletcher, Elkin & Co. Trinity wharf, Woolwich, & at Commercial wharf, West street, Gravesend
Glasscock John Laybank, Causeway, Bishop Stortford
Hardy & Doughty, Cowley mill wharf, Uxbridge moor
Harris Stephen, Iron & slate works, Kingston
Hawkins & Co. Magdalen street, Colchester
Hawkins Charles Henry, Magdalen street, Colchester
Johnson W. St. John street, Chichester
Lock William, Strand street, Sandwich
Longley G. the Hall, Preston,Faversham
Longley J. 34 St. Geo.'s pl. Canterbury
Osborne, Stevens & Co. High street, Uxbridge
Ritchie & Smith, Ravensbourne wharf, Greenwich
Robinson Andrew Augustus (late Thomas Stirling), Bow bridge slate works, Stratford
Sadd John & Sons, Market hill,Maldon
Smart W. 32 Chapel street, Worthing
Smart W. G. H. Tarrant st. Arundel
Smith H. G. Albion wharf, Greenwich

Extract from the Post Office Directory of Essex, Herts, Kent, Middlesex, Surrey and Sussex, 1855.

over 100 people from the area. John Hide bought the mill in 1889, and the family continued to run it until 1955, when it was bought by Stephen Walters & Co. from Suffolk. In 1985 the then owner, Ede & Ravenscroft, which still makes robes and regalia, sold the buildings to Hampshire Buildings Preservation Trust and it is now the home of Whitchurch Silk Mill Trust. Some silk weaving is still carried out today (see below for contact details). Overton, not far from Whitchurch, had its silk mill with eight workers' cottages nearby.

Kent could have been the centre of the southern silk industry if the silk mill opened by George Courtauld and Peter Nouaille in Sevenoaks had been successful. Instead, the pair quarrelled and Courtauld left, eventually moving to Braintree in Essex. Nouaille stayed in the area, however, where he and his family continued the silk mill, which became known as 'Greatness'. East Sussex Record Office has apprentice indentures that frequently mention Nouaille as taking on pauper youngsters and Canterbury Cathedral Archives has deeds that include notes relating to the leasing of property to Nouaille & Co., cambric manufacturers in 1772. However, Sun Insurance company records at the Guildhall refer to him as a crape manufacturer, so it would appear that the mills produced a number of different fabrics. By the mid-nineteenth century the family had become part of the 'gentry'. A number of their wills can be found at The National Archives documents online. At Lullingstone Castle, Kent, a silk farm was developed as late as the 1930s, producing silk that was used for Royal events. Later, this firm moved to Dorset. Some of its business records from 1932–1955, together with various leaflets about the farm, have been deposited at the Mill Green Museum and Mill in Hatfield (see below).

Pirn winder, Paradise Mill.

Centred on the villages of Blockley, Broadway and Winchcombe, the silk industry survived in the Cotswolds until the end of the nineteenth century. There are references to silk mills and silk throwsters in deeds at the Gloucester Record Office and two silk throwsters (James Smith and Edward Banbury) are referred to in the deeds of Blockley School, dated 1858. The Baptist church at Blockley records its first baptism in 1821 as being in the 'mill pond attached to the silk mill occupied by Mr C Smith'.

Stretching from Derby down to Matlock Bath along the Derwent Valley, mills in this area include the first 'factory' of its kind – Lombe's silk mill. In 1704 Thomas Cotchett, a retired solicitor from Derby, established a silk mill on Little Island in the River Derwent. This was not successful and he went bankrupt in 1713, but in 1715 one of his employees, John Lombe, with his brother Thomas, bought the building and commissioned George Sorocold to build a larger mill on the site. The Lombe brothers brought in new machines based on ones from Italy, which were water powered. It was this early decision that ensured that silk spinning and knitting were centred on Derby.

Shortly after this, in 1743, Charles Roe opened his silk mill in Macclesfield and before the end of the eighteenth century the centre of the silk industry had followed. There were more than a hundred silk mills in the town, with others in the surrounding districts. Paradise Mill, which first began producing silk in 1862, was taken over by Messrs Cartwright & Sheldon just before the First World War and remained a hand-weaving mill until its closure in the 1980s. It now houses the Silk Museum, with many working machines exhibited and still producing small amounts of silk. Around the area you can still see the workers' houses, with their typical third storey for the looms before they were all brought together into the factory.

Towards the end of the nineteenth century competition from Eastern countries and changes in fashion produced a gradual decline in the silk industry. Around Coventry the silk weavers had produced mainly silk ribbons. One of these, Thomas Stevens, turned his skill in producing ribbons to the production of silk bookmarks. This later developed into silk portraits and postcards, which became known as Stevengraphs. Other firms quickly followed suit. Two Macclesfield firms, J & T Brocklehurst and William Whiston & Son, merged to form Brocklehurst Whiston Amalgamated and began to produce woven silk pictures. Pattern books for this company, and many other silk firms, can be found at the Silk Museum, Macclesfield.

Weavers' houses, Macclesfield.

The silk trade had its own union, the Macclesfield Power Loom Silk Weavers' and General Silk Workers' Association. This eventually became the National Silk Workers' Association, until in 1965 it merged with the Amalgamated Society of Textile Workers and Kindred Trades. Records, which principally relate to the workings of the union, have been deposited in the Working Class Movement Library in Salford.

Many textile areas had at least one silk mill, the yarn being mixed with other fibres, particularly worsted, to give a high-quality fabric.

Chapter 9

THE WOOL INDUSTRY

The quality and type of wool depends very much on (a) the sheep from which it comes – northern hill sheep produce shorter, coarser fibres, whereas southern sheep produce wool of a longer, finer staple, and (b) the section of the sheep on which it grows – there are a variety of names for these types of wool, varying from region to region.

The fleece is first divided up or sorted into different qualities depending on staple length, fineness of the wool and so on, which will affect how the wool is finally used. Sorted wools are then blended with other wools of a similar quality.

Willeying was originally a hand process to clear the wool of debris, but machines were quickly invented to shake out all the dust and dirt from the wool and to loosen the fibres before scouring, which involves washing the wool to remove its natural grease, dirt and impurities. The wool then has to be dried. From scouring, the grease, 'lanolin', is sold on to other industries to be used in the making of soap and cosmetics etc.

To be used the wool has to be straightened out, or carded, so that all the fibres lie in the same direction. Originally done using two cards, rather like a pair of ping-pong bats covered in tiny metal hooks, the carding machine not only straightens the fibres but also removes any remaining vegetation from the wool. At the end of the process the wool has become a soft, rope-like length called a sliver.

Worsted cloth uses the longer, finer staple. The wool is carded, washed again then combed to separate out the shorter fibres, called noils, which can then be used in woollen production. The longer fibres can be wound into a ball, known as a top.

The nap on the cloth was raised, initially by hand using small 'bats' on which were stuck teasel heads. Once the nap was raised, men using croppers – huge iron clippers sheared the nap off to produce a finer finish to the cloth. The final finishing could include the application of various chemicals and dyes.

In the middle of the fourteenth century came the Black Death, decimating the population and creating a labour shortage. Agriculture began to change from the labour-intensive, cereal-based system to sheep farming. Foundations such as Rievaulx and Fountains in Yorkshire, Furness in Lancashire, Margam and Tintern in Wales and Ely in Cambridgeshire were built, all of which found sheep farming an ideal method of producing income. Kirkstall Abbey near Leeds is reputed to have owned thousands of sheep and Leeds soon grew to be the centre of a medieval woollen industry, providing transport and a market for the cloth.

Wool produced by the abbeys was exported all over Europe via their nearest port. Annually 8 million fleeces were exported from Britain, sent out as raw wool and returned later as cloth woven by the more expert weavers in Belgium, France and Italy. In the north, York became

Fountains Abbey, Yorkshire.

the main centre, sending wool down the River Ouse and out to the northern European countries and Scandinavia. In the south, the Italian merchants from Lombardy and Florence preferred to deal with the ports of London and Southampton. The West Country and Midlands increasingly exported their wool through Exeter and Bristol. In the thirteenth century the woollen trade was dominated by Flemish merchants, then later by Italians. However, such was the wealth English wool created for the country that Edward III commanded that the Lord Chancellor should sit on a sack of raw wool in Parliament to remind him of how important the trade was – and the woolsack is still there to this day.

When, in 1353 Edward III imposed a duty on each sack of wool, known as the Ordinance of the Staple, some 'Staple' cities such as Winchester, grew considerably, only to decline in importance when collection of the tax was transferred, in the 1360s, to Calais itself. The Fellowship of the Staple, which governed the export of wool and collection of taxes, became a very powerful, rather closed community. Some clothiers rose to wealth and renown. Thomas Stocker, of Wyboston, Bedfordshire, was a wool merchant during the fifteenth century and his son John became one of the wealthiest wool merchants in England. His nephew, Sir William Stocker, became Mayor of the Calais Wool Staple and Lord Mayor of London. This latter appointment was extremely brief. Sir William was appointed Lord Mayor on 24 September 1485, being sworn in two days later. Two days after that, on the 28th, he died, never having reaped the benefits of his prestigious appointment. However, Richard Whittington, who was a wealthy cloth merchant, was more successful, becoming Lord Mayor of London in 1397, 1406 and 1419.

The production and export of wool during the Middle Ages created wealth that funded the building of large and ostentatious buildings, some of which survive, such as in Cranbrook and Tenterden, Kent. Many of Suffolk's prettiest towns and villages bear witness to the wealth of the medieval wool trade. Timber-framed buildings, fifteenth-century guildhalls and narrow cobbled streets abound at Hadleigh, Kersey and Bildeston. Lavenham is probably the best known of all the Suffolk towns for its collection of medieval buildings. Norwich, too, had its wealthy merchants, such as Robert Toppes who occupied the Dragon Hall, now fully restored. Many churches, known as 'wool' churches, were built on the proceeds of the sale of wool. Wool from Oxfordshire was in high demand because of its quality and there was

Dragon Hall, Norwich, built in about 1430.

a major wool market at Chipping Norton, which helped fund the building of St Mary's Parish Church there. The Cotswolds have many 'wool' churches, such as that of St Peter and St Paul at Northleach or St James' at Chipping Campden. In fact, many towns throughout the country have some evidence of wool merchants providing churches or having elaborate tombs inside the local church. Effigies and brasses often show a wool sack or lamb in recognition of this source of wealth. John Kendrick of Reading, a wealthy clothier and merchant with contacts all over Europe who became mayor of Reading in 1565 and an Alderman of London, left a large sum of money to purchase a building, called The Oracle in Minster Street, to support clothiers in the area. Records relating to Kendrick's charity can be found in Berkshire Record Office. The Oracle was demolished in the nineteenth century.

The main wool-producing areas at this time were the Cotswolds, Leicestershire and East Anglia, where the sheep produced a long staple, fine wool. Lincoln became a large city with a population of over 10,000, many of whom were employed in the wool industry. Dyes were imported, particularly from the Mediterranean, while the finished cloth was exported all over Europe. Unfortunately, Lincoln specialised in shades of russet and red, especially the shade that became known as Lincoln Scarlet, and by the end of the fourteenth century this had gone out of fashion. Within a very short time the weavers had left. Some of the larger estates continued their sheep and wool production but the wool tended to be exported for the cloth to be made on the continent. The Lincolnshire textile industry became a cottage affair, done alongside other occupations such as farming, and the wool merchants moved away to other major towns with better transport links.

For some towns, wool products became of such importance that the whole area depended on it. In the area now known as Cumbria, not only was cloth made, but woollen stockings and other small knitted goods were produced and taken to the local markets at Kirkby Stephen, Kirkby Lonsdale and, most importantly, Kendal. Kendal took the motto 'Pannus Mihi Panis', meaning 'cloth is my bread' because it was of such importance to the wealth of the town.

Medieval Lancashire provided small amounts of cloth for local use or for sale in the counties round about. The wool used tended to be coarse and was not in demand in Europe at this time. During the fifteenth century Parliament eventually exempted these suppliers from having to ship wools through the Staple port of Calais because the value was too low to bear the charges. This enabled the small cloth manufacturer to continue to make a living as an independent trader, despite a general depression in the industry in the mid-1400s, affecting many of the older, town-based industries. Trade moved inland to smaller towns or villages where some capital was available and water power for the fulling mills, and where the influence of the trade guilds were weaker. Bristol was fortunate in that it was a port, taking in wool from South Wales, London, Southampton and from all over the south west for export, as well as manufacturing cloth. As early as 1346 Bristol had its woollen guilds, which regulated the trade, but as manufacturing moved away, export links were established throughout Europe – for wool up to the fifteenth century, and for cloth, as well as imports of wool and dyes, up to the nineteenth century. Many people also migrated through this port over the years.

The fifteenth century saw the rise and fall of the Merchant Adventurers – merchants who banded together and came to dominate the export trade, particularly cloth exports to Europe. The Company of Merchant Adventurers of London was founded in 1407 and the Guild of the Mistery of Mercers of York in 1430, trading particularly with northern Europe and the Baltic. Studies of the records for the York Merchant Adventurers Company have been published by the Borthwick Institute (see p. 175) and include, D M Smith's *The Company*

Merchant Adventurers House, York.

of Merchant Taylors in the City of York: Register of Admissions 1560–1835, 1996 and Anna B Bisset's *The Eastland Company, York Residence: Register of Admissions and Register of Apprentices 1642–1696.*

The Company of Merchant Adventurers of Newcastle, founded in 1547, was granted a licence to collect wool throughout the north of England for export to Germany, the Baltic and other north European countries. According to www.british-history.ac.uk, the original officers named on the charter of incorporation include Henry Anderson, Governor; Robert Brandling, Robert Lewen, George Davell, Mark Shaftoe, Cuthbert Ellison, Robert Brigham, William Carr, Bartholomew Bee, Roger Mitford, Thomas Bewicke, Bertram Anderson and Oswald Chapman, Assistants; Bertram Bewicke and John Rawe, Wardens. The records, found at Tyne and Wear Record Office, include apprenticeship indentures, member accounts, copy wills and deeds and correspondence.

When Henry VIII destroyed the power of the monasteries in 1538 the lands were sold off. Wiltshire and Swindon Archives hold a number of documents relating to the sale of Malmesbury Abbey to

William Stumpe, who was born in North Nibley in Gloucestershire, but became one of Malmesbury's wealthiest merchants. After buying the Malmesbury Abbey buildings, he installed a number of looms, thus becoming one of the earliest factory owners.

In 1614, James I, in need of more money, agreed to withdraw all the privileges previously granted to the Merchant Adventurers and gave them instead to William Cockayne, who had persuaded the King that he would export more English cloth and therefore raise further revenue. Within a few years Cockayne's business collapsed and the privileges were restored to the Merchant Adventurers, but by that time the damage had been done. The English cloth trade lost many of its European markets and some of the clothiers who were producing cloth went bankrupt, causing great hardship in local areas.

Much of the Baltic trade was under the control of the German Hanseatic League (the Hansa), which was a Confederation of over 150 north European cities, such as Breslau, Cologne, Hamburg, Krakow and, most importantly, Lubeck. Many merchants had trading houses in London, the most important being in Steelyard, which had its own warehouses and church as well as merchants offices and houses. This became the centre of London's commerce. All these 'aliens' operated in London, thus many people whose ancestors were connected with the merchants may find they have European links in their family. The tremendous power of the Hanseatic League gradually declined as trade routes changed and they were officially expelled from London in 1598.

With few means of communication, one of the most important medieval sales methods was the yearly fair, which was strictly controlled, often disrupting the lives of the town's citizens for the duration of the fair, but also leaving records in the form of Pipe Rolls and other legal documents. St Giles' Fair at Winchester, strictly controlled by the bishop's men, was held for sixteen days in August. It attracted merchants from all over, particularly London, wool being sent from York, Beverley, Lincoln, Leicester and Northampton, as well as from all over Europe. A 'great fair' was also held at Northampton from the twelfth century onwards for which cloth buyers came from Europe but especially Scandinavia and Holland. Darlington, Boston and St Ives had important fairs. At Smithfield, near St Bartholomew's Hospital, London, the annual cloth fair became known as Bartholomew Fair until it ended in the nineteenth century

At Stourbridge Fair in Cambridge one particular section, known as the Duddery, after the coarse cloth worn by many poorer people, was given over to the wool trade and Defoe, journeying round England in 1724, described it:

> clothiers from Halifax, Leeds, Wakefield and Huddersfield in Yorkshire, and from Rochdale, Bury, etc, in Lancashire, with vast quantities of Yorkshire cloths, kerseys, penistones, cottons, etc, with all sorts of Manchester ware, fustians, and things made of cotton wool; of which the quantity is so great, that they told me there were near a thousand horse-packs of such goods from that side of the country, and these took up a side and half of the Duddery at least; also a part of a street of booths were taken up with upholsterer's ware, such as tickings, sackings, Kidderminster stuffs, blankets, rugs, quilts, etc. In the Duddery I saw one warehouse, or booth with six apartments in it, all belonging to a dealer in Norwich stuffs only, and who, they said, had there above twenty thousand pounds value in those goods, and no other.

The importance of these fairs gradually declined as communication and other means of selling developed.

The Midlands

In the Midlands, the hand-knitting frame was introduced in Leicestershire, building on the wool-production industry that was already in existence there. The knitting frame was used to produce hosiery, which became the principal manufacture, using local wool from the Leicestershire sheep. Leicester, Loughborough, Hinckley and Castle Donington became the main centre of the hosiery trade. Richard Mitchell was one of the first to build a factory in Leicester, opening a steam-powered establishment in 1851. In 1865 Edwin Corah started building St Margaret's Works, which eventually employed over a thousand people, but closed during recession in the 1970s.

Developments in the cotton-spinning industry were soon transferred to the woollen industry. Coltman, Whetstone & Brookhouse of Leicester became one of the first partnerships to take advantage of the new machinery to produce worsted. However, violence from workers who felt it threatened their way of life caused such disruption that in the late 1780s the local corporation banned the machines. This was very much to the benefit of other areas, such as Yorkshire, which was quick to take up the advantages of the new machines.

The textile industry seems to have reached a peak in Northamptonshire in the mid-eighteenth century, followed by a sharp decline that was probably due primarily to the development of a mechanised worsted spinning industry in Yorkshire and Leicestershire. According to recent research (published on the following website: www.geog.cam.ac.uk/research/projects/occupations/abstracts/paper5.pdf) the textile industry was largely concentrated in the north-western part of the county, particularly Rothwell, Corby, Huxloe, Guilsborough and Spelhoe. The militia lists show that Kettering had a number of weavers, woolsorters and dyers, suggesting that there was a thriving woollen industry by the end of the eighteenth century, but in other areas there is little evidence of widespread, full-time occupation in textiles.

The South West

Devon's early cloth industry, using local, relatively poor-quality wool, produced cloth known as 'Tavistocks' or 'straits'. The Exeter Company of Weavers, Tuckers and Shearmen was formed here in the fifteenth century, and the records (1292–c. 1940: charters, title deeds, leases, minute books, certificates of admissions, lists of freemen, accounts, correspondence re property and accounts of charities) are in Devon Record Office. Crediton was one of the main markets for the area at this time, but some of the cloth was sold in London, enabling the merchants to become quite wealthy. A small textile industry existed in Cornwall from the fourteenth century onwards. The wool produced was very poor quality, known as 'Cornish hair' and used to supply a local market rather than for export. It is known that cloth was produced at Truro, Launceston and Cosawes, where there was a wool factory (Manor of Cosawes records can be found at Cornwall Record Office).

In north Somerset the industry fragmented. Bath, specialising in woollen manufacture, was the central market town for its surrounding villages and along the River Avon. Frome concentrated on dyeing cloth, using woad grown in the area to produce a blue cloth, which was used for military uniforms. Shepton Mallet mainly produced woollen stockings.

The Dutch immigrants influenced the making of cloth, often referred to as 'new draperies' due to being lighter and therefore not as hard-wearing – a boon to the textile industry. English weavers quickly adopted these new methods. As the early wool-producing industry declined, the south west 're-invented' itself to become the foremost cloth-producing area, importing its wool from other areas in England but also from Europe. Small clothiers, though, were still the norm – men who owned small workshops adjoining their houses, with just a few looms and a number of outworkers who worked in their own cottages. By the sixteenth century, the change from the export of raw wool to exporting cloth brought an increase in the number of English merchants.

By the beginning of the nineteenth century blankets were being made in Newbury, Berkshire, and it is probable that John Coxeter, who was a well-known manufacturer from Whitney, owned Greenham Mills. It was here that he took on a wager to produce a coat from shearing to wearing in a day. In fact he did it in just over thirteen hours and the coat can still be seen at Coughton Court, Alcester, Warwickshire.

The south west saw a gradual increase in mechanisation, and the industry continued to grow, though much more slowly than in its medieval heyday. The earlier export of kerseys reduced and more worsted, stockings and flannel were sent abroad instead. New cloth, known as serge, began to be produced during the seventeenth century, which led to an expansion of the trade. Tiverton and Exeter were the main Devonshire areas producing this cloth, as well as Totnes and Ashburton, where fulling mills were built near the river. One of these was Gages Mill, which later produced flock for mattresses until it closed and became a private residence. Some deeds relating to this are in Devon Record Office. The East India Company had a monopoly on the Chinese tea trade and as such could force the Chinese to buy English cloth. The Company bought large amounts of cloth from the south west, bringing prosperity to many of the towns. One of these was Ashburton, which supplied cloth to the East India Company, but the town declined when the East India Company lost its monopoly in the mid-nineteenth century and ceased buying cloth. Textile workers moved away to other areas or into other trades. Tavistock, which had previously been involved in the wool trade because of its Abbey, also contributed for a few years to the cloth exported, but by the nineteenth century copper had become more important. Exeter was the centre of the export trade, most of the cloth from the south west leaving from this port. It is possible that this trade was influenced by an influx of Flemish weavers and, in about 1700, textile workers known as the 'poor Palatines'. In the Devon Record Office there is correspondence relating to these refugees and 'mentioning that Mr Dix of Exeter has proposed to employ 4000 to 5000 Palatines in the manufacture of flax and tow near Torbay'.

By the mid-nineteenth century the woollen trade in Devon was being badly affected by the northern counties and the majority of mills closed. One enterprising agent, Thomas Bury of Exeter, even advertised in the *Leeds Mercury* in 1818 offering his services as factor to 'any northern manufacturer who wished to use the Devonshire markets to buy or sell wool and cloth'.

There were woollen mills around Probus during the nineteenth century and Perranarworthal was home to Lovey's manufactory, but little apart from deeds remains for these. Field names and will records suggest that there were some mills around Truro, such as the one at Grampound, near Truro. Here a small spinning and woollen mill was certainly in existence at the beginning of the nineteenth century, but had burnt down by 1835.

Blamey's Wool Mill, owned by J H Blamey from Liskeard, continued into the twentieth century when it was taken over and now it is occupied by Devon & Cornwall Wools. The whereabouts of the company records, however, is unknown.

The very wealthy mill owners had a large influence on the area – for good and bad. Edward Sheppard and his son Edward ran a large mill at Uley in Gloucestershire, employing the majority of workers in the village. When, in 1837, the firm went bankrupt all those workers were thrown out of work and looked to the parish for support. Some details can be found in the poor-law records of the time but emigration was encouraged. Many moved to other parts of the country, others went abroad to America, Australia and South Africa, leaving the village decimated. Reports of the bankruptcy appear in the *London Gazette*, as well as local papers, and details of the property for sale also give names of those who were in occupation. For example, on 26 May 1837, the notice includes details of:

> A capital stone-built mansion house . . . in the occupation of the Reverend Marlow Watts Wilkinson . . . a cottage thereon, occupied by Shadrach Jobbius, George Smith, and George Dauncey. . . . Three cottages, near the last-mentioned, 'with

Outlets, occupied by Thomas Bushell, Ludby Sherwood, and. John Brooks. . . . Closes . . . in the occupation of James Haile and John Norris. . . . A leasehold cottage and garden, at a place called Ginfield, occupied by George Hale, held for the residue of an absolute term of 1000 years'.

As production of broadcloth in the south west declined, Wiltshire turned to the lighter, fancy cloth production. The first years of the nineteenth century were particularly traumatic for this area. Machinery was being brought in and the shearmen (known as croppers in the north) lost their skilled, highly paid jobs. During 1802–1803 there were many attacks on mills, wrecking the machinery and cloth made on them. Newspapers of the time give many details of the mills attacked and the firms in them. There was considerable correspondence between the south west and Yorkshire at this time. George Palmer from Yorkshire had travelled in the west and knew many in Trowbridge. When magistrates started intercepting letters, the shearmen began sending correspondence by courier. Eventually, as events escalated Littleton Mill was burned down and a youth named Thomas Helliker was, supposedly, recognised as being there. At his later trial in 1803 the Yorkshire group paid £100 towards the cost of legal support for him and others arrested. The judge, Simon Le Blanc, was later to preside over the Luddite trials in Yorkshire.

Once steam power came to the area, more mills were built and cloth production flourished until the beginning of the twentieth century. The last mill, Salter's Home Mill, closed in 1980 but one of its mills became the Trowbridge Museum. Records for Samuel Salter & Co., which range from 1769–1982, include corporate, financial, production, staff and wages records etc.; c. 1790–1930: deeds and business papers can be found at Wiltshire and Swindon History Centre. At the Wiltshire & Swindon Record Office factory inspector's registers for Salter's include: the register of young persons under 18, giving name, address and date of first employment, certificates of fitness for employment for those under 16, giving parents' names, date of birth; records of accidents giving personal details and cases of poisoning or disease.

The Cotswolds

The heyday of the wool industry in Gloucester was probably the Middle Ages, when wool from the Cotswolds was in demand all over Europe. The industry gradually moved from the valleys, where villages such as Berkeley and Thornbury declined, towards the southern Cotswolds where there was greater water power for fulling mills and other machinery. Stroud, Nailsworth, Minchinhampton and Avening all grew immensely, with mills lining the valley sides. The area became famous for its scarlet cloths, specialising in broadcloths, which required heavy fulling. This material was often used for military uniforms and, later, for billiard and snooker tables. This change also gave rise to large-scale mills and wealthy mill owners putting the small clothiers out of business. Newspapers from the nineteenth century carry many advertisements for sales of machinery and other items. In 1825–1826 there were many meetings, rallies and riots over the changes in the industry, particularly the use of machinery. These events are covered in the newspapers, but also Quarter Sessions records show who was prosecuted.

The Playne family was involved in textiles from the early eighteenth century when they leased Longford Mill, not far from Avening in Gloucestershire. By the mid-nineteenth century two brothers, Peter and William, were in control of two mills there, but in about 1820 the partnership split up – Peter moved to Dunkirk Mill in Nailsworth and William continued in Lake and Longford Mill, where he built up a successful business producing striped material for the East India Company. In 1920 Playne's joined with Hunt & Winterbotham and Strachan & Co. of Lodgemore Mills to form Winterbotham, Strachan & Playne Ltd. Later Kemp & Hewitt joined Playne's in Longford Mills. Winterbotham, Strachan & Playne Ltd later became part of Illingworth Morris of Bradford (Bradford Archives have a brochure with material sample and a brief history of firms in the group, including William Playne and Co. Ltd, Longfords Mills; Reid and Welsh Ltd, Lossiebank Mills, Border region; Salts (Saltaire) Ltd; Samuel Salter and Co. Ltd, Home Mills, west of England; Strachan and Co. Ltd, Stroud; Hunt and Winterbotham, Cam Mills, west of England; Kemp and Hewitt Ltd, Trowbridge, Wiltshire). Longford Mill closed in 1990 and has since been converted to houses and apartments. Lodgemore Mill was originally a fulling mill but converted to cloth. It is still in use today by Milliken Ltd, making cloth for snooker tables and sports equipment.

The Marling family started as small clothiers, rising to become wealthy baronets. Records mainly relate to the family, though the partnership deeds survive from 1825–1866. However, Sir William H Marling wrote a treatise on the woollen industry of Gloucester in which he mentions many families, including Anthony Fewster of

Nailsworth, Captain Slade of Uley, Peter Playne of Dunkirk and David Ricardo of Gatcombe, who all provided funds for assisted emigration from the area. He specifically refers to sixty-eight people who emigrated from Bisley at a cost of £191 3s 1d in August 1837. He also refers to a local habit during this time of stealing bits of wool, known as 'slinge', from the mills and selling it. Eventually, the manufacturers took action and prosecuted, often leaving records that appear in the Quarter Sessions.

A very detailed description of all the mills and their occupiers in the Nailsworth valley can be found in British History Online: 'Nailsworth: Economic history', *A History of the County of Gloucester: Volume 11 Bisley and Longtree Hundreds* (1976), pp. 211–215; www.british-history .ac.uk/report.aspx?compid=19112. This work also refers to many flock and shoddy mills in the area. As the woollen industry began to move northwards, some businesses tried to diversify. Mills producing shoddy were opened but the industry as a whole did not expand in the south west and soon centred on Dewsbury and Batley in the West Riding. Few records remain for these businesses, but reference to them may be found in deeds, apprentice records, newspapers and bankruptcy records.

Other towns involved in the textile industry include Cirencester, which had a small carpet industry, and also experienced an exodus of many workers to Kidderminster in about 1836. Bristol was both a production area and a port for the wool.

There were close links between Banbury and London, where cloth was exported to France, and Southampton, which exported cloth to Italy. Records for families involved can be found through wills, deeds, leases or ulnage accounts, held at The National Archives.

By the eighteenth century the wool industry as such had declined but there was still an important manufacturing industry around Banbury. The area was particularly noted for shag or plush fabric, which was extensively used to make uniforms for household staff, such as footmen. It was also used as upholstery material. Well-known names involved in the trade include George Green and King, Snow & Howarth, which both appear in the trade directories of the 1790s but not thereafter. Most of the mills in the area used handlooms and the industry could not compete with the power looms used in the north and Midlands. Many factories had closed by the early twentieth century, some moving to Coventry and often taking part of their workforce with them.

Oxfordshire took advantage of new markets in America and Africa, supplying blankets to cotton- and sugar-plantation owners. When a Weavers' Guild was set up in the eighteenth century, they built a blanket hall and all blanket cloth had to be taken there for sale, thus providing some local protection for the industry.

Some of the later blanket manufacturers include Smiths Blankets (Witney) Ltd, set up in the 1850s, the records (1926–1973) for which are to be found partly in Oxfordshire Record Office. Other records (1925–1956: minutes, corporate and financial records) are in Manchester Local Studies and Archives as part of the archives of N Philips and Co. Ltd, which bought a large interest in the company in 1926 and James Walker & Sons, a Yorkshire firm that decided to open a factory in Witney after a legal ruling that only blankets made in Witney could be called 'Witney' blankets. They built their factory in 1933 but eventually closed in 1980, though their mill in Mirfield, Yorkshire, still operates today.

Probably the most famous blanket manufacturer in the area was the firm of Early & Co. The family are known to have been in the area in the seventeenth century and various members of the family seem to have been involved in the textile industry and working as manufacturers by the nineteenth century. By the 1860s the firm of Charles Early & Co. brought all the family businesses together, becoming a limited company at the beginning of the twentieth century. At the start of recession, in the 1960s, when many amalgamations took place, the firm merged with James Marriott & Sons. This business in turn became associated with Courtaulds. In the troubled years at the close of the twentieth century the firm eventually went into receivership. The records of the company are held at Oxfordshire Record Office, but one of the original blanket looms can be seen at Farfield Mill in Cumbria. A number of the Early family wills can be found at The National Archives documents online.

Mop making derived from the blanket industry as a way of using up the waste wool and this industry survived in Oxfordshire until the general decline of textiles in the twentieth century.

At Shutford, just outside Banbury, Robert Lees, who appears in trade directories of the mid-nineteenth century, opened a plush mill, continuing in partnership with the Gillett family until 1848. Other firms associated with this area include William Wrench & Co. and Cubitt & Son. Oxfordshire Record Office has a newspaper report about the mill when it closed in 1948.

The Gillett family was concerned with banking as well as textiles. Setting up a small factory at Brailes, they eventually moved to Banbury, where they were involved with the plush factory at Shutford. The Gillett collection of papers at Oxfordshire Record Office includes many items relating to the plush industry in the area, as well as deeds and agreements by various members of the family in their manufacturing business and partnerships. A set of index cards gives names, ages and sometimes the address of persons connected with the textile industry, including weavers, of linen, plush, shag, web, worsted, mohair, stocking and sacking, dyers, lace makers, yarn winders and wool combers.

The weaving of horsecloths and making of girth webbing seems to have been prevalent around Oxford, beginning as early as 1700 and continuing into the twentieth century, when the firm of H and F Ford, which also made ropes, closed in 1944. Another manufacturer, T R Cobb, also involved in banking, sold his mill in 1870. The business then changed to making tweed. Some records of the firm can be found in BT31 at The National Archives, which refers to the dissolving of earlier companies – the Banbury Woollen Tweed Company in 1876 and Banbury Woollen Manufacturing Co. in 1901. Later the Banbury Tweed Company was formed and this firm continued until 1932.

The Bliss Tweed Mill, run by William Bliss & Co. of Chipping Norton, was built towards the end of the nineteenth century, making tweed and employing large numbers from the nearby town until its closure in 1980. For access to its records, contact The National Archives.

The South East

Guildford seems to have begun its association with cloth after the settlement of Flemings in the fourteenth century and still retains some of the old weavers' cottages. However, the industry survived only until the seventeenth century. Records rely on ulnage accounts (at The National Archives), property transactions and wills for individuals rather than business records. Surrey History Centre also has an undated petition of the clothiers of Guildford to the Commissioners for Trade concerning the wool trade and cloth industry in the town. Petitions often include signatories.

The East

While eastern England was extremely important for its production of wool, by 1800 much of the wool trade was beginning to migrate north.

Many businesses tried to diversify and produce silks, drabbets (a mixture of linen and cotton) and cotton goods. In Haverhill, Suffolk, where the Wool House was built in the mid-seventeenth century to help in the trading of wool products, Daniel Gurteen set up a textile business making fustian cloth. The Gurteen family were very influential in the town, funding the building of many institutions. In 1856 they built Chauntry Mill from where they still operate today, making menswear. A second mill followed in 1865. By the end of the nineteenth century they had moved into horsehair weaving, following this with the weaving of coconut fibre. By the beginning of the twentieth century they had built a new factory run by steam power.

Norfolk, particularly Norwich, was an important centre for worsted, possibly named after the town of Worstead, where many Flemings settled during the sixteenth century, or possibly after the Dutch name for the fabric – Ostade. The immigrants had to apply to the King for special letters of protection since they were often the victims of violence perpetrated by the local inhabitants. However, they brought their weaving skills with them and soon new fabrics were being made in England. The Worsted Weavers Guild was active during the fifteenth century, but it is believed no detailed records survive. Around Maidstone and Canterbury the new fabrics were developed and the older woollen areas of Kent declined. Reference is made to the cloth industry in early deeds and Canterbury Cathedral Library and Archives hold a list of Canterbury freemen 1700–1750, various deeds and apprentice records but there are no company records extant.

Norwich had been an important cloth-producing area and made 'Norwich stuffs', a lightweight worsted that needed extensive finishing, and Norwich Shawls, made from silk or a mixture of silk and wool, which were considered to be the finest available. Norwich Red was a popular dye produced in the town principally by its inventor, Michael Stark, who had dye works there. Shawl production employed large numbers of people until its gradual decline during the nineteenth century as fashions changed.

The next few hundred years saw distinct changes in the various regions of England and Wales. As steam power spread, the production of textiles moved away from the rural areas and into the towns, moving also from the south of the country to the north, which was well supplied with coal and iron. In Wales, workers often migrated from the surrounding counties in England as well as Wales to work in the Flintshire mills. Later, when the mills declined they migrated out to the textiles areas of Lancashire and Yorkshire. Women particularly took this route – working in the mills gave them a much higher wage than many other occupations. These migrants were predominantly from the northern Welsh counties. Further south, migrants would often travel to the Midlands, though they too may have then moved up to the north, following jobs. Land-tax records, tithe maps and the duties on land values books of 1910 may produce some information about land use and occupation, but few are indexed.

The North West

Lancashire became well known for 'small wares', such as ribbon and laces, but there was also a large number of cloth manufacturers, particularly around the Manchester area. Broadly these can be divided into the coarse cloth known as rugs (still a cloth, not a floor covering) and friezes, which tended to be a long length of about 36yd and about $3/4$yd wide, produced in the Manchester, Bolton, Rochdale and Bury area and the shorter, lighter kerseys made around the north-eastern area of Blackburn, Burnley, Colne, Padiham and Preston. A cloth known as 'Manchester cottons' was also produced and there has been considerable debate as to what this was. It was certainly not cotton, as we would use the term. Some have said it was a mixture of wool and linen since the cloth was lighter in weight than the coarser cloths. It has been suggested that cotton – known then as cotton wool – was used but where the raw material came from or who wove it is not known. Will inventories from the area do not seem to include cotton, though other materials are listed. It is probable that the cloth was all wool and the term 'cotton' simply referred to its lightweight and softness or possibly because they looked like the cotton cloth manufactured in Europe.

The North East

In the north east the wool industry gradually declined, though some coarse fabrics continued to be produced. Some woollen and worsted yarn and cloth manufacturers were still operating in the area up to the 1830s, though by the mid-eighteenth century few were left. The reasons for this decline are varied. Competition from other areas of the country as the Industrial Revolution took hold, increased competition for local capital which could bring better returns from investments in coal or steel and the lack of an effective, cheap, transport system in the area all played their part. Paton & Baldwin Ltd, an amalgamation of a Scottish and a Halifax firm producing knitting wools, opened factories in Jarrow and Billingham before the Second World War, and a further factory in Darlington when the war ended, moving its headquarters there too and eventually employing over 4,000 workers (though 2,000 workers lost their jobs in Halifax when the mill there closed), gradually declining over the years as the industry shrank. In 1961 the company became part of the Coats Group. The records for this company are in different archives. Of the original companies, one was John Paton & Son of Alloa and another J & J Baldwin and Partners of Halifax. Some records are in West Yorkshire Archive Service, Calderdale. Other records are at Clackmannanshire Archives, Alloa Library, 26–28 Drysdale Street, Alloa, FK10 1JL, Scotland; tel: 01259 722262; email: libraries@clacks.gov.uk; website: www.clacksweb.org.uk/dyna/archives.

Yorkshire

The principal change came in the eighteenth century when the worsted industry moved away from Norwich to the West Riding. There is much debate about the reasons for this, the two main suggestions being that water-powered machinery was being introduced to the industry and the fast-flowing streams of Yorkshire were more suitable for the new technology and that there was a more enterprising attitude in the north. Many workers from the eastern counties moved to the north during this time, bringing their skills, and families, with them. The end of this century saw the Industrial Revolution really start to take hold, bringing immigrants from Ireland, from counties around Yorkshire and from the rural areas into the towns, turning the industry from a cottage-based one to a factory based one. Though outworkers still existed, they no longer worked for themselves, but were employed to work in their own homes by the factory owners.

The textile industry in Yorkshire changed too. There was a distinct move away from the eastern towns to the West Riding, particularly Halifax, Wakefield and Leeds, where the small clothiers combined cloth production with farming to bring in a second income. York and Hull gradually specialised in commercial enterprises and acted as the major ports for the county, but Ripon and other towns declined as a result of the move to the west. This was the first era of the display of

The gravestone of Robert Watson, a damask weaver, at Bedale, North Yorkshire.

wealth through building and many clothiers built themselves extensive houses or funded public buildings, just as they would later do in the nineteenth century. Monuments and gravestones can also be found, such as that of Robert Watson, a damask weaver of Aiskew who was not only able to pay for an inscribed gravestone in Bedale churchyard, but also left fascinating details (in North Yorkshire Record office) of how to set up a loom for a variety of patterns. The Dales became famous for knitted products, mostly stockings, caps and gloves. One group even became known as 'the terrible knitters of Dent' because they could knit so quickly, but most village women (and men) knitted for themselves and for sale to earn a second income.

Gradually there was a concentration of wool and worsted production in the West Riding and a massive increase in output, but it eventually declined towards the end of the twentieth century. Growth in population during this time was phenomenal, many towns doubling in size in just a few years. Leeds, Halifax, Huddersfield and Bradford all became highly industrialised. The West Riding is the area most people think of when they talk about the Yorkshire textile industry. Grazing for sheep, fast-flowing streams for waterpower, with coalfields for steam-powered machinery, canals and railways linking the area with ports at Hull, Manchester and Liverpool as well as south to London helped provide the infrastructure, while a long-established textile industry provided expertise. Migrants came from all over the world to the West Riding, but different towns developed and specialised in different ways.

Bradford was part of the early cotton industry, as well as developing large-scale mills during the nineteenth century. Cotton mills were built here, spreading from Lancashire, though many later converted to worsted. Bradford retained a spread of textile production but its primacy was in white worsted, becoming the centre for this type of fabric. Wool consumption in Bradford rose from over 1 million pounds weight in 1810 to over 6 million pounds weight by 1825 (Firth, *Bradford and the Industrial Revolution*). Bradford's Piece Hall became the foremost selling place for plain worsted, attracting merchants from around Yorkshire but also particularly from Germany. Many merchants moved to Bradford and one district, now a conservation area, is known as 'Little Germany'. Many of the records of these merchants are in Bradford Record Office and include correspondence from all over Europe.

Memorial to the victims of the accident at Newland Mill.

After about 1830 dyeing became important in the town, the biggest manufacturer being Ripley & Sons. In 1882 there was a terrible accident at the company mill, Newland Mill, when the chimney fell on the works. Some records for this accident, plans of the buildings and apprenticeship indentures are at WYAS, Bradford. The Bradford Dyers' Association was set up in 1898 in order to buy up the businesses of various companies and firms engaged in the Bradford/Yorkshire piece-dyeing trade. Records for this Association are in Bradford Archives.

Bradford was also home to one of the largest alpaca and mohair producers – Sir Titus Salt. Having made his fortune, Sir Titus built his own mill in a new village called Saltaire, surrounding it with workers' housing, schools, churches and meeting houses. The only building missing was a pub as he was a strict teetotaller. In 1960 Salts was taken over by Illingworth Morris but the mill became almost derelict before being restored in 1987. Salts Mill and the village of Saltaire is designated a UNESCO World Heritage Site. Some later business records from the 1920s and those of the Salt charities, such as schools and hospitals, are to be found at Bradford District Record Office.

Detail from the plaque on the statue.

Statue of Samuel Lister, Lister's Park, Bradford.

Unfortunately, there are no earlier records, nor any relating in detail to workers, but census records show who was living in Saltaire and would therefore probably have been employed in the mill.

Samuel Cunliffe Lister owned Manningham silk mills as well as others and the firm employed 11,000 people in the 1870s. On his retirement Lister sold his parkland to Bradford and this is now known as Lister's or Manningham Park.

After the Second World War and particularly in the 1960s many people from all over the Indian sub-continent came to this area to work in the textile mills. The factories often wished to open round the clock, with women working the day shifts and Asian men working the night shifts. When the industry went into decline, many Asian families found all their breadwinners out of work. Some used redundancy money to set up their own businesses and have been very successful. The Local Studies Library, Bradford Central Library, has a collection of over 700 interviews reflecting Bradford's past, including many with those from different ethnic backgrounds.

Halifax was one of the most important textile areas in the eighteenth century, the trade growing to such an extent that a specific building was needed for the purpose. A small cloth hall was built but in 1779 the Piece Hall was opened. The hall was divided into small units that could be rented by the weavers, but this practice gradually fell into disuse as larger mills sold cloth direct to the merchants. The Piece Hall is now a heritage centre with shops.

Piece Hall, Halifax.

As the town's textile industry developed Huddersfield began to produce fine-quality worsted cloth rather than the lower-quality cloth made in Bradford, culminating in the amalgamation of a number of firms into Huddersfield Fine Worsteds, centred on Kirkheaton mills. Records for these firms are in Kirklees Archives. In addition to high-quality worsteds, Huddersfield specialised in fancy waistcoatings in many different patterns. Since many of these fabrics required a variety of different yarns in their making, there has always been a range of yarns produced in the area, including cotton, silk and speciality yarns. Design also became important, some firms (particularly nowadays) eventually specialising in design while the cloth was produced elsewhere. Many firms had contacts throughout the world and regularly exhibited at trade fairs. Details of winners often appeared in local newspapers.

Heavy woollen district

This was so called because the recovered wool was generally used in making 'heavy' coatings and duffels and blankets. When cloth had reached the end of its useful life, rather than just be thrown away the rags were recycled. Machines were invented that could grind woollen waste, breaking it up and enabling it to be re-spun into 'new' wool. Using the soft rags that had previously been stockings, carpeting or flannel gave rise to 'shoddy' wool. Later it became possible to recycle worsted rags in the same way – this being known as 'mungo' and was slightly better quality. Much of the rag material was imported. As Germany put a high duty on the export of rags, branches of Yorkshire firms were set up in Berlin and the resultant reclaimed wool imported instead. Trading links with Europe were quite close at this time and migrants came and went with the trade.

Batley and Dewsbury were the acknowledged capitals of this particular trade. Fabric made using part shoddy or mungo and part new wool was inferior in quality but much cheaper. Other areas that had large numbers of shoddy mills include Heckmondwike, which specialised in producing blankets, Elland, Morley as well as Ossett and Gomersal, which made a slightly better cloth, particularly for the Army and Navy. Many other towns also had some shoddy and mungo dealers who would collect rags and offcuts from the mills to take to be recycled.

Most of the archives in the area have records relating to shoddy and mungo concerns, for example the records of J T and J Taylor, woollen manufacturers, Blakeridge Mill, Batley, at WYAS Wakefield, include a 'Spinners' day book', giving details of individual spinners and work done 1829–1831.

In the eighteenth century Leeds grew rapidly and cloth was brought from the towns round about, including Wakefield, Halifax and Huddersfield, to the cloth halls for sale to European merchants. Cotton mills were also built at this time, initially water powered but Leeds was quick to take up steam power. This led to early concern about the effects of smoke and action was taken against the worst offenders. In May 1824 Benjamin Gott was prosecuted because of the pollution created by smoke emissions from his mills, and he was put on trial in York. The case was dismissed on the grounds that his mill had been there first so the builders knew about it when they constructed houses nearby. The *Leeds Intelligencer* carried a full report of the trial.

Benjamin Gott's Bean Ing mill in Leeds was one of the earliest and largest in Europe. He employed thousands of workers, using about £350,000 capital at a time when most mill owners needed only £50,000. He was one of the first to bring all the manufacturing processes together into his own mill. Another mill belonging to Gott is now the Industrial Museum at Armley.

By the end of the nineteenth century many Jews fled Europe, arriving in England via London or Hull, intending to journey on to America. Many did, but some remained, particularly in Leeds and Manchester where they became an important part of the textile industry. Leeds was already well known for its finishing trade but the influx of Jews provided an impetus to expand the tailoring trade. After Meshe Osinksy arrived in Britain from Lithuania he changed his name to Montague Burton and eventually opened a tailoring factory in the city after the First World War. He employed over 15,000 people and operated a welfare and pension scheme for his workers. The firm still exists as part of the Arcadia Group. Some archives have been deposited at Leeds Record Office. Others, relating to various properties, are with the record office where the properties were situated. Search A2A for details. The BBC produced a documentary on the firm as well as a programme entitled *The Jews of Leeds*, videos of which are in WYAS, Leeds.

Wales

In north Wales fulling mills were able to take advantage of the streams for water power. The Welsh for fulling is 'pandai' and these mills are

Newtown Flannel Exchange.

often referred to as 'Pandy' mills. Their prevalence is reflected in the number of towns and villages that have 'pandy' as part of their name. There are sometimes references to fulling mills on many of the larger estates, but finding family details would involve searching through estate records, none of which are indexed.

The making of flannel was always been a cottage industry in Wales, much of it being produced in Welshpool and Llanidloes until the mid-nineteenth century, when the industry became centred on Newtown. Buyers, many from England, bought from the market here. Power looms were introduced in about 1850 and many mills were built or extended. The general depression in the industry in the 1830s caused much unrest and in 1839 riots in the town were quashed by troops who occupied the town for almost a year. Many textile workers and others who had taken part in the riots were sent to prison or transported. Reports of these events appear in the newspapers, Quarter Sessions and prison records. The fortunes of many Welsh woollen mills have been tied up with other major industries – mining and iron works. Both involved heavy, dirty work that necessitated constant washing of clothes. Flannel was strong enough to stand up to this usage and so

Page from a Cardiff trade directory with entries for wool merchants, 1914.

local mills supplied their own area with the cloth. When the heavy industries declined, so did the textile industry. In Bala the local industry was knitting stockings. These were exported across Europe until, in the nineteenth century, the stocking industry in the North and Midlands developed and took over their markets.

In 1874 the Welsh Flannel Manufacturing Company, which eventually became the Holywell Textile Company, took on two mills in Holywell. Production continued until 1922 when Courtaulds took them over. They renamed the mills 'Deeside Mills', and continued working them until 1989. Some of the remaining buildings are currently being renovated for use as craft workshops. For records for the Welsh Flannel Manufacturing Co. Ltd, Holywell, Flintshire, 1877–1980, contact The National Archives.

The Teifi Valley was one of the most important areas for the woollen industry. Mills were found all along the valley and into the town, though only the ones in the rural areas are still in existence. Rock Mill at Capel-Dewi is one of the last working water-powered wool mills in Wales. Dre-fach Felindre, now home to the National Wool Museum, was a major centre for producing wool, flannel and tweeds for both local use and export. Woollen mills at Talybont had introduced machinery by 1835 to compete with the northern mills. Leri (Lerry) Mills and Ceulan Mill prospered until the end of the nineteenth century. A gradual decline then set in with Ceulan Mill closing in the 1950s, but Leri Mills hanging on until the 1980s. Reports of these closures appear in the local newspapers. Records for some of the businesses can be found at the National Wool Museum. Carmarthen Record Office has some records relating to Bargod Woollen Mills, run by John Jones from about 1886 to 1921.

Further south was a small-scale woollen manufacture, with early fulling mills mentioned in estate collections. But in 1900 there were twenty-six woollen mills in the county of Pembrokeshire. Valley Mill near Fishguard dates back to the eighteenth century. When it was sold in 1912 it was renamed Tregwynt Mill. By constantly changing its products the business weathered the storms of the twentieth century and is still in production today. Solva Mill, not far away in St David's, is another mill that has survived by diversifying, changing from producing woollen fabrics to carpeting and is still in business. The water wheel is being restored, but no documentary records remain. Evidence of workers may be found in census records, Quarter Sessions or overseers' accounts etc.

The heyday of the Welsh textile industry came after the eighteenth century when newspapers were beginning to be published. For example, the *Cambrian* began in Swansea in 1804, the *North Wales Gazette* in Bangor in 1808 and the *Carmarthen Journal* in 1810. These were weekly journals but in 1861 the first daily paper, the *Cambria Daily Leader*, was published in Swansea. Daily newspapers in particular carried details of local events, mills opening or closing, accidents or outings. A useful website is www.newsplanwales.info/s002.php, which can be used to find which newspaper covered a particular area or the specific holdings of a library or archive.

The National Library of Wales at Aberystwyth holds a large collection of documents and books relating to Welsh family history – often items that in England would be in the local record office, so it is often worth looking at their website catalogue even if your ancestor came from some distance away.

Chapter 10

OTHER TEXTILE MATERIALS

Hemp is a bast fibre (i.e., produced from a plant stem) similar to flax. It was used for canvas, webbing, sailcloth, sacking, rope and for the base of carpets.

Jute is a plant-based material similar to hemp and is used in a similar way. The main centre of the jute industry is now in Scotland, but the London Jute Manufacturing Company opened its factory in 1865, though it closed in 1882. Some records of the dissolved company are at The National Archives in BT31. In 1874 the managing director was Captain D R Clarke, with William Young as manager. Other works included a matting factory and John Scadlock's steam-dye works at Bylocks Hall. He also had a branch in Islington, London. At Stratford-le-Bow in 1864 William Ritchie & Sons employed about a thousand people in their jute factory.

Ramie is made from the stems of Chinese nettle and initially prepared in a similar way to flax. Though it is a tough material, it is also highly inflammable, often used in making gas mantles. It could be used as a warp yarn for wool and linen cloth.

Coconut fibre is known as coir, now principally used for doormats, but has been used for making bags, brake linings and rope etc.

Sisal, a plant that gives a strong yarn used in rope making, is also called sisal hemp. William Armes set up a matting business in King's Lynn in 1830 using coir and sisal. In 1888 he moved to Chilton Mills in Sudbury. With the advent of plastics, the firm began producing mats woven from PVC, before being taken over in 1969 by the Guthrie Corporation, although the family regained control in 1985.

Rayon is a vegetable yarn, sometimes known as artificial silk. By the end of the nineteenth century, scientists across the world were working on the production of an extruded yarn that could be cut to any length or used as one long filament, like silk. In 1894 British inventors Charles Cross, Edward Bevan and Clayton Beadle patented their version, which became known as viscose rayon. The New Artificial Silk

Spinning Co., based at Wolston near Coventry, was formed, but it went into liquidation in 1900. Courtaulds bought the rights to the technology in 1904. At first the quality was too poor to be viable, but eventually the quality of the cloth, produced at Halstead Mill in Essex, improved and sales soared.

Glanzstoff Manufacturing Company opened a factory in Flintshire, Wales, in 1908 but, being a German firm, it was taken over during the First World War by Courtaulds. The factory was re-named Aber Works. Courtaulds had other mills in this area, eventually employing over 10,000 people in the area. The population of the area rapidly increased to staff the factories, so Courtaulds, like many other large textile businesses, built houses for their employees. These included Swinchard Walk, which mostly housed managers, Evans Street, Henry Taylor Street and Dee Cottages. Some records for these works are to be found at Flintshire Record office (1910–1973: Castle Works reports, accounts, wages books, registers of young persons, factory inspection records and papers), together with some relating to the Aber Works.

Mohair is from the angora goat and is often used as hand-knitting wool. Alpaca, llama, vicuna, huanaco or guanaco are all types of South American goat, the hair from which was used extensively in a variety of cloths. Cashmere is another goat, this time from the Himalayas, which has a soft, fine hair particularly noted for its warmth. It began to be used in Britain after about 1800 with the rise of the British occupation of India. Used particularly for shawls, it is difficult to dye, but wool was often treated to give it a soft 'cashmere' finish.

Camel hair is not shorn but plucked by hand from the camel during moulting in summer. Short, downy body hair is soft and warm, being used for making blankets or dressing gowns. Camel-hair cloths are some of the most expensive cloths produced.

Horsehair is taken from the mane or tail. The best quality is made into braid, haircloth or stiffening fabrics. Others are made into lower-quality cloths and covers. Horsehair was a material much used in Victorian society and many towns had a manufacturer or dealer. A factory was built in Bells Lane, Glemsford, Suffolk, in about 1820, apparently by the parish officers, to provide employment for paupers. It was later occupied by Arnold & Gould (Horsehair) Ltd from the beginning of the twentieth century until a few years ago, when it appears to have closed down. Many people were employed here – washing, hackling (combing) and forming the hair into bundles ready for sale. Some records, including staff records, are in Bury St Edmunds Record Office.

In Castle Cary, Somerset, John Boyd Textiles produce horsehair cloth on handlooms dating back to 1870. The business was established in 1837, moving into Higher Flax Mills in about 1850. Horsehair often used cotton or silk warps and was used extensively for furnishings. Some records exist, including share records and financial books. For access, contact The National Archives. As far as it is known, this is the only horsehair factory still in existence.

Chapter 11

OTHER BRANCHES OF TEXTILES

11.1 Machine hosiery manufacture

Originally hose (close-fitting leggings or breeches worn by men) was knitted by hand and was very much a cottage industry, principally done by women and children. Many workers had a frame in their own home and used the work to supplement their income from other jobs, such as farming or labouring. As demand increased, they became full-time framework knitters, but as fashion changed and trousers became the norm, the industry gradually declined.

Knitting frame, Masson Mills.

In 1589 William Lee invented a knitting machine specifically for the hosiery industry. When Queen Elizabeth refused him a patent for the machine, he moved to Rouen, France, and began manufacturing there. After his death his brother, James, returned to England and built machines in London. Eventually, to try to establish some control over the industry, James Lee helped set up The Worshipful Company of Framework Knitters, which received its charter from Oliver Cromwell. This applied initially to the industry around London, but in 1663 its influence spread nationwide. Only after a seven-year apprenticeship could anyone enter the trade and deputies were appointed to oversee the important East Midlands districts. A need to expand the industry gradually brought about the Company's demise and by the mid-eighteenth century its function became primarily social.

The knitting industry spread out from London, developing in the East Midlands early in the seventeenth century. As well as local sales, goods were exported to the continent and even as far away as the West Indies, but the industry was still run on a 'cottage' basis. The East Midlands continued to have strong links with the London markets and many firms opened their own warehouses in London in order to sell their goods and sons were often apprenticed to London merchants.

The beginning of the nineteenth century was a time of hardship and major changes in the textile industry. In the Midlands the knitting industry was hit by changes in fashion that reduced demand for knitted stockings. Workers, threatened with loss of employment, blamed the machines, the attitude of the machine owners and the growth of the use of 'cut and sew' hosiery (stockings that were knitted flat and then sewn up with a seam at the back). Their anger flowed over into the 'Luddite Riots', which spread throughout the Midlands and up into Yorkshire and Lancashire. For the next few decades the area suffered a series of poor years, with unemployment, low wages, riots and ill-feeling between employers and employees, interspersed with good years, when rates were raised and workers were reasonably well off. Gradually, the 'outwork' system declined and the knitting frames were moved into larger workshops or factories, which eventually became steam driven.

The Leicester knitting industry specialised in worsted products. Over the years, the framework machinery moved from the homes into the mills and became water, then steam, operated. I & R Morley developed into a large business, with a number of factories throughout the East Midlands and by 1886 employed almost 10,000 people. In the 1960s it became part of Courtaulds.

'Out' or 'home' work continued, despite the rising number of factories. Even in 1900 many firms still had thousands of domestic workers, some of whom, known as 'cheveners', embroidered designs on socks or stockings.

In Nottinghamshire one of the most successful businessmen in the eighteenth century was William Elliot (1702–1792). He appears to have come from the London area and set up, initially using outworkers, embroidering patterns on stockings, before eventually building mills in the area. He developed a black dye for silk stockings, was knighted and died a very rich man, leaving his fortune to two nephews, who continued in the silk industry and built a number of silk mills in the area. His life story is recorded at the Brewhouse Yard Museum, Nottingham (see Chapter 13).

When, in 1764, James Hargreaves invented his 'Spinning Jenny', which enabled a single spinner to spin eight (and later up to 100) threads instead of just one, many workers perceived it as a threat to their livelihoods. To avoid the machine breakers, Hargreaves moved his business to Nottingham, setting up a mill in Hockley to produce cotton yarn. Richard Arkwright, too, aware of the need to produce good-quality yarn for the hosiery industry, also moved to Nottingham. The cotton hosiery industry was firmly established in the East Midlands area.

11.2 Rope, twine and sailcloth making

Rope can be made from a variety of fibres, but traditionally natural fibres, such as sisal, cotton, jute and hemp, were used.

The rope maker worked at the 'rope walk', where the fibre was spun into yarn. Fibres were attached to a single hook on a wheel, which was slowly turned, twisting the fibres together. The rope maker walked back down the 'rope walk', which could be 300ft or more long, depending on the length of rope required. As he walked he fed out more fibres from the bundle he carried. The wheel twisted the fibres together into strands and then a number of the strands were tied to hooks attached to a twisting machine and run to a single hook on a 'sledge'. As this wheel was turned, the strands were twisted together to form the rope.

Many towns had rope makers, but the majority were found in coastal towns, providing rope for the shipping industry. By 1827

Rope making, Bewdley, Worcestershire.

Sunderland had sixteen rope makers, while Stockton had half a dozen, as well as four sailcloth makers. In South Shields there were seven rope makers. Michael Corbitt and Sons Ltd, rope and sail manufacturers, were established at Hebburn and Robert Percy Sanderson of The Ropery, Silksworth Lane, Bishopwearmouth, continued making ropes into the early twentieth century.

Many companies also amalgamated and therefore records may not be where you expect. In 1924 British Ropes Ltd was formed by a merger of nine different companies, including R Hood Haggie & Sons of Newcastle. British Ropes later changed its name to Bridon Plc. Takeovers and mergers continued until the 1970s. Though much of its production was in wire rope, other divisions made fibre-based ropes and binder twine for agricultural use. Some of the records for this company and its subsidiaries are at Doncaster Record Office, but permission is needed to view them (contact the archivist for this).

In Hampshire, ropes and sails were supplied to the shipbuilding yards at Portsmouth. A mill at Criddlestyle produced sailcloth using flax, then converted to a woollen mill until its closure in 1954, but no records appear to remain. Emsworth had a range of textile-related industries primarily linked with shipbuilding, including rope making for the Portsmouth Dockyard.

Mention the Isle of Wight and yachting inevitably comes to mind, so it is not surprising that the main link with the textile industry relates to sail making. The firm of Ratsey & Lapthorn was established here in the nineteenth century before moving to Gosport. The Gosport Museum contains a section on sail making and includes this firm in its display.

Devon, too, had many small businesses connected with the sea. A number of deeds in the Exeter Record Office refer to rope manufacturers, such as John Stephens of Budock, or to sailcloth manufacturers, such as Peter Dyer, whose will was proved at the Bishop's Court in Exeter in 1809.

Flax and hemp were grown extensively in Dorset, giving rise to the related industries of rope and twine manufacture, sailcloth making, sacking and netting, all of which were used in the local fishing industry and the Navy as well as being exported. There was a strong link between this area and the Canadian fishing industry around Newfoundland.

Bridport was one of the main centres for net and twine manufacturing, with over fourteen firms in existence there by the end of the nineteenth century. The Hounsell family were involved in the industry from the seventeenth century onwards, owning a variety of mills and companies. Over the following fifty years many of these amalgamated: William Hounsell & Co. Ltd, Herbert Hounsell & Co. Ltd, Ewens & Turner and Richard Tucker & Sons merged to form Hounsells (Bridport) Ltd.

At the same time, William Edwards & Son merged with Thomas Budden & Son and Albert Norman & Son. Rendall & Coombs Ltd merged with William James & Co. in 1939 and at the end of the Second World War joined with W Edwards & Son (Bridport) Ltd, later including William Gale & Sons.

Bridport Industries Ltd was formed in 1947, buying out both the Hounsell Group and the Edwards Group. In 1963 Joseph Gundry & Co. Ltd merged with Bridport Industries Ltd to form Bridport-Gundry Ltd. Records for all these companies are at the Dorset History Centre. There is also a Sound Archive, which includes some 'rope and net industry' interviews, and a number of photographs of flax workers in fields.

At Burton Bradstock large flax mills were built in the mid-eighteenth century by Richard Roberts, who had developed a worldwide flax and hemp business by the end of the nineteenth century. Despite this, few records remain. Dawe's Twine Works was built at West Coker, using the local flax to produce ropes, twine and canvas. In 2006 a campaign was begun to restore the building.

Wills and deeds in both East Riding Archives and Hull City Archives often refer to sailcloth and rope manufacture, sacking or bass (baskets for the docks) makers.

Whitby's linen industry manufactured sailcloth, but also made ropes and sackcloth.

Few records remain, apart from occasional apprenticeship indentures, such as that of John Walker to Thomas Chilton, sail maker of Whitby (a photocopy of which is at the Whitby Literary and Philosophical Society), and evidence of trade directories and census returns. Other ports such as Scarborough also had small-scale sailcloth and rope makers. Hall's Barton Ropery Company Ltd was incorporated in 1936 but actually began making fibre ropes in about 1767 at Barton-on-Humber. It closed in 1986 and some records survive. Some, relating mainly to running the company, are in East Riding Archives and these include the Articles and Memorandum of Association.

Rope making was carried out in farming districts too, the rope or twine being needed for baling hay and straw or for a variety of tethers and reins for animals. Thomas Wharton, rope makers, was established at Hawes, a central market for the surrounding Dales, by the early nineteenth century. The Wharton family continued in business until it was sold in 1905 to W R A Outhwaite. The name W R Outhwaite & Son continues, though the business has since changed hands again and is now owned by P and R Annison.

Ropes, tents and tarpaulins were made extensively in Oxfordshire. The firm of Wall & Co., under various members of the family, survived from the eighteenth century until about 1940. Some of their records, mainly ledgers, account books and order and day books, can be found at the Department of Special Collections and Western Manuscripts, Bodleian Library, Broad Street, Oxford OX1 3BG; email: reader.services @bodley.ox.ac.uk; website: www.ouls.ox.ac.uk/bodley/library/ specialcollections.

A useful website for information on the making of ropes is: www.rope-maker.com/index.html.

11.3 Carpet and rug manufacture

The term carpet can be used to describe any kind of woven floor covering. Rug usually refers to smaller carpets, often handmade by hooking strips of cloth or thick yarn through a tough, open-weave cloth.

Carpets can be produced in different ways:

- Woven – on a loom in a similar way to cloth but with heavier yarn. Often highly patterned. Early flat-weave carpets were also known as tapestry weave or double cloth.

- 'Brussels weave' – this was made by weaving the backing (usually of cotton and jute) and at the same time including pile yarns looped over wires or rods inserted across the width. The wires were then simply withdrawn, leaving a loop.

- 'Wilton' – this method included knives on the wires or rods and, as they were withdrawn, they cut the pile, hence 'cut-pile' carpets. A variety of patterns can be created using this technique. The yarn can be given different twist strengths, or loops can be cut evenly, unevenly or a mixture of cut and loop pile.

- Tufted – developed in 1930s, tufted carpets use a totally different technique. Tufts are individually fixed in a backing material using needles. The backing is coated with a sticky compound to secure the tufts and usually a second backing is added to improve the carpet strength. Originally, tufted carpets tended to be in single colours or printed with a pattern after production.

While most cottages would have had their rag rugs, the industry was very much home based, but in 1655 a carpet factory was built at Wilton, forming the basis of the carpet industry in this country. At this time carpets were flat woven, similar to the 'ethnic-style' rugs that are becoming popular again. Another method was of hand knotting strands of wool on to a loose grid of strong warp and weft. Once again, refugees from the continent brought weaving skills with them and soon became the mainstay of the industry.

In 1701 William III granted a protective charter to weavers in Axminster and Wilton to help the small carpet industry. The Earl of Pembroke and Montgomery brought European carpet makers to work for him. Two Frenchmen, Antoine Dufossy and Pierre Jemale, were put in charge and it was Dufossy who, in 1749, developed a method of cutting loops on the carpet weave to make a nap that became known as Wilton carpet. In 1755 Thomas Whitty established a carpet-making business in Axminster and Brintons, previously a cloth producer, began making carpets in the Midlands in 1770.

Thomas Whitty's carpet factory at Axminster supplied wealthy families throughout the country with specially designed carpets. The company continued for a number of years after his death, run by various members of his family. Some family papers and probate details can be found in the Devon Record Office. The mill was burned down and rebuilt in about 1835; shortly after this, the firm closed and all business was transferred to Wilton in Wiltshire. However, in 1937 Harry Dutfield, a carpet manufacturer from Kidderminster, another major carpet-producing area, opened a carpet factory in Axminster, thus reviving an old tradition. In 1950 the firm, now named Axminster Carpets Ltd, acquired a mill in Buckfastleigh as a spinning and dyeing plant and later expanded into New Zealand. It is still in existence and the records are believed to have been retained by the firm. A major carpet museum is currently being developed in Kidderminster (see Chapter 13).

The north east, too, had its carpet industry, centred on Barnard Castle. As early as 1815 Thomas Crampton switched from cloth manufacturing to carpets, and by 1827 there were five factories employing about 600 workers. Walter White in his tour of Yorkshire in 1858 describes Barnard Castle as having 'just beyond the green, a mill of cheerful chatter' (White, *A Month in Yorkshire*). Monkhouse & Co. of Thorngate, Smith & Powell and Hepworth's all operated in the town,

Thorngate Mill, Barnard Castle.

though by 1874 their combined workforces had been reduced to fewer than 200.

In 1598 Henry Smith of Durham fell out with his daughter and left the bulk of his estate to the City 'for charitable purposes', to provide employment for young men and relief for those too old to work. The legacy included various premises, so the trustees decided to buy further properties and over many years loaned money to various entrepreneurs to set up and run 'cloth-working trades' to provide employment and training for the poor of the area. Few of these ventures were successful until John Starforth, a local weaver, 'set up and effectually carried on the manufactory . . .' (Shea, *Carpet Making in Durham City*). By the end of the eighteenth century he was employing over 700 workers in the area, initially in weaving linen cloth before moving to carpets and woollen cloth. However, by 1805 the firm had become bankrupt, many blaming the effect of the French wars.

In 1814 Gilbert Henderson moved his business, and many of his workers, from the village of Church Merrington to Durham, into Starforth's original premises and began an association with Durham that lasted almost a century. By the mid-nineteenth century Durham had become the third-largest carpet-producing area in England, continuing production despite price wars and a general decline in the industry. However, in 1903 Henderson's closed its door. A few members of staff were offered employment by Crossley's of Halifax, which had bought out the assets of the firm, but most lost their jobs.

Hugh Mackay then started up on a small scale, the business surviving and expanding up to the beginning of the Second World War, when all carpet production was stopped and jobs switched to making Army blankets and other supplies. After the war, carpets were again made but during the general decline of the textile industry in the 1970s the firm moved out of Durham City to cheaper premises. In 2005 the factory closed.

In Darlington, the Kipling family had been weavers of linen cloth but started weaving carpets in about 1813. As the linen industry declined, more and more of the production was switched to carpets. In Pigot's 1828 Directory, Francis Kipling & Sons is listed as a linen and carpet manufacturer, but by 1855 was purely producing carpets. The firm closed in about 1860.

In addition to many other branches of the textile industry, Halifax became one of the foremost production areas for carpets. A number of firms established themselves in the area – Webster's at Clay Pits,

William Currer at Luddenden, Job Lee at Lower George Street, Halifax, and Abbott and Ellerton at Halifax. The firm that had the most influence was John Crossley's, established in 1803 and eventually moving into Dean Clough Mills. By 1864 John Crossley & Sons had branches at Kidderminster, as well as Halifax, and warehouses in London and Manchester. At one time the firm employed over 2,000 people. In 1953 and 1969 they merged with carpet firms in Kidderminster to form Carpets International. However, the decline experienced in the 1970s saw a gradual reduction of the workforce and eventually production moved to Kidderminster and Dean Clough closed in 1987. There are extensive records for this firm, and its subsidiaries, at Calderdale Archives.

The Crossley family were very much involved in the local township, providing the People's Park and also setting up Crossley Orphanage (changed to Crossley & Porter Orphanage when Thomas Porter contributed to the funding). This eventually became Crossley & Porter School, later Crossley Heath School. Records of the orphanage are at Calderdale Archives.

11.4 Leather manufacture

The skins first need to be washed and the remaining hairs and fat removed. It is then treated with chemicals to turn it into leather (known as tanning). The chemicals can then be removed and the leather treated to soften it before being dried. Originally, the process was done with tannin from oak bark in special bark mills. The leather might then be treated with other chemicals such as alum to produce soft kid leather for use particularly in making gloves.

Many areas had small tanning works, but larger establishments could be found in Mitcham, Surrey. Here George Drake and Sons, William Webb and John Deed & Sons all had extensive leather factories during the nineteenth century. There was a tanning mill at Gomshall, latterly owned by the Bray family. Some records relating to this can be found in the Surrey Record Centre with the Bray family papers. The mill continued in use until the 1980s when it closed.

In the latter part of the nineteenth century Northamptonshire and Leicestershire both developed very important boot and shoe industries that became major employers. Although a hundred years later the industry was hit by the general decline and most factories closed during the 1970s.

Norwich became famous for quality shoes. James Smith established his manufactory in Norwich in the late eighteenth century. His small business eventually developed into a large concern, now named Start-rite and still operating in Norwich.

Staffordshire had a thriving shoe industry until the twentieth century. Lotus Shoes moved from Derbyshire to Stafford in 1814, eventually becoming one of the biggest employers in the town. In 2005 a Boot and Shoe Community History Project was begun which collected oral histories from people who had worked in the factories. This is now available in book form from Staffordshire Record Office.

Walsall's leather industry concentrated on production of saddles and bridles, turning later to 'small' goods such as wallets. A useful website is: www.walsall.gov.uk/index/leisure_and_culture/leather museum/history_of_leather.htm.

11.5 Hatting

Felting is the process of matting the wool fibres together using water and pressure until a fabric is formed. Raw wool can be felted on its own, but usually it is knitted or woven into fabric first and then fulled by hand by 'walkers' who walked the material in vats or, later, in fulling mills using water power and massive wooden hammers.

Later hats were knitted then felted afterwards. Felting was a cottage industry, the hat often being made by the men, shrunk to the required size and finally trimmed by the women.

Wool is not the only material that is used in making felt hats. Fur, generally rabbit but sometimes beaver, was also used. In the fourteenth century the beaver fur came from Europe or Russia but as the animals became almost extinct in Europe, the fur was imported from North America. In making hats from beaver fur, the pelt had to be brushed with a solution of nitrate of mercury. Mercury fumes cause brain damage, hence the expression 'mad as a hatter'. Stockport's fur felt-hat making industry became established during the seventeenth century, developing from a cottage industry to a major factory based industry by the end of the nineteenth century. There is a Hat Museum in Stockport (See Chapter 13).

The straw-hat making industry was initially a cottage industry and carried out alongside other work or by elderly or very young women. The straw was used whole, which gave a very coarse result so the better hats were imported from Italy, where a method of splitting straw had been developed. However, during the Napoleonic Wars imports were unavailable so the home industry expanded. Edward and Thomas Waller developed the industry, particularly around Luton. The straw was flattened and split, then woven into plaits, which could be stitched together to make hats and bonnets. By 1800 plaiting schools were being set up to give a basic education and teach plaiting skills, although these quickly died out with the advent of the national system of education in the 1870s. Weekly plait markets were held at Luton, Dunstable and Hitchin.

Cheap imports from the 1870s eventually ended the plait market, but the industry continued for many years. In 1878 Edmund Wiseman invented a machine that could sew plaits, rather than these having to be sewn up by hand, which led to the work being undertaken in factories rather than at home.

Sanders and Brightman, Currant and Creak Ltd and Lye and Hubbard, the latter producing felt hoods from about 1920, were all based in the Luton area. The Vyse Hat Factory was founded in 1764 by Thomas Vyse, a French immigrant. On 25 February 1930 a massive fire broke out in the factory in Bute Street, Luton, killing eight people. The factory was rebuilt and production continued to 1956, when it was moved to London. Details of the fire and its victims appeared in the newspapers of the time. The firm finally closed in 1977. Some hat manufacturers still remain in the area – Bermona and Walter Wright & Co. in Luton and Failsworth Hats of Manchester, which took over the Luton-based firms of Marida Ltd and S G Parker. An Easter Hat Parade in Luton has recently been revived as a local festival.

Other areas where the hat industry established itself include Southwark, particularly noted for the use of beaver fur, which was very fashionable in the middle of the nineteenth century. R and R Whitehead & Brothers, felt manufacturers, had a factory at Mitcham, Surrey, in 1891, though this was later closed and production continued in the company's Lancashire mill. Some of their records are held at Oldham Local Studies and Archives, but for share and staff records access contact The National Archives.

Chapter 12

RECORD OFFICES BY AREA

12.1 National sources

• The British Library, St Pancras, 96 Euston Road, London NW1 2DB
• British Library Newspapers, Colindale Avenue, London NW9 5HE
• The British Library, Boston Spa, Wetherby, West Yorkshire LS23 7BQ; website: www.bl.uk.

Records are available to view, with a reader's pass (obtainable from the library on production of two forms of identification, which include name, address and signature, and an application form), in the reading rooms at both the St Pancras and Colindale addresses. However, Colindale is due to close in 2012 when the documents will be moved to Boston Spa. There is an ongoing project to digitise the collection. There are plans for a microfilm copy to be available at the St Pancras branch.

The national newspaper library includes many magazines and periodicals from Britain and some foreign publications. It also holds a large collection of patents, trade marks and designs, maps and other manuscripts. There is an online catalogue.

• Modern Records Centre, University Library, University of Warwick, Coventry CV4 7AL; tel: 02476 524219; email: archives@warwick.ac.uk; website: www.warwick.ac.uk/go/modernrecordscentre.
There are collections relating to named businesses, trade unions, employers' and trade associations. There is an online catalogue.

• The National Archives, Kew, Richmond, Surrey TW9 4DU; tel: 02083 925200; email – see the contact addresses on the website; website: www.nationalarchives.gov.uk.
The repository for archives throughout the country, The National Archives has a number of printed guides that can be found on their website. Those of interest to anyone searching for textile ancestors include:

- Apprenticeship Records as Sources for Genealogy
- Bankruptcy Records After 1869
- Bankrupts and Insolvent Debtors, 1710–1869
- Business History, Sources for
- Companies and Businesses: Registration
- Customs' Accounts, Medieval
- Immigrants
  - Jewish History, Anglo-Jewish History, 18th–20th Century, Sources in The National Archives
- Labour History, Sources for
- Markets and Fairs
- Taxation Records Before 1689
- Wills and Death Duty Records After 1858
- Wills and Probate Records
- Wills Before 1858: Where to Start

In addition, there are a number of general family history guides to the holdings.

The website www.nationalarchives.gov.uk/archon/ links to ARCHON, which gives contact details for all record repositories in Britain and some organisations abroad that have collections relating to Britain.

The website www.a2a.org.uk/ links to Access to Archives, a searchable database giving details of collections in archives throughout Britain.

The National Register of Archives contains information on the nature and location of manuscripts and historical records that relate to British history. This can be searched by corporate, personal, family or place name. It gives lists of holdings and repository details; website: www.nationalarchives.gov.uk/nra/default.asp. To search the specific collection of business and corporate archives online by company name access the website: www.nationalarchives.gov.uk/nra/browser/corporate/corporatehome.htm.

The Manorial Document Register includes information about manorial documents, but only information relating to Wales, the Isle of Wight, Hampshire, Norfolk, Surrey, Middlesex, the three Ridings of Yorkshire, Cumberland, Westmorland and Lancashire north of the sands (the Furness area, part of Cumbria since 1974) is available online. For other areas, you will need to visit the search room or send a written enquiry; website: www.nationalarchives.gov.uk/mdr/.

Some records have specific restrictions on them. Details of means of access can be obtained by writing to The National Archives.

• National Monuments Record, Enquiry & Research Services, English Heritage, National Monuments Record Centre, Kemble Drive, Swindon SN2 2GZ; tel: 01793 414600; email: nmrinfo@english-heritage.org.uk; website: www.english-heritage.org.uk/nmr.
Holds some records relating to buildings and has an online photographic collection .

• People's History Museum, Manchester, The Pump House, Left Bank, Bridge Street Manchester M3 3ER; tel: 01618 396061; email: info@phm.org.uk or admin@phm.org.uk or archive@phm.org.uk; website: www.phm.org.uk.
The museum traces the development of worker movements – many of which developed out of the industrialised areas.

• Society of Genealogists, 14 Charterhouse Buildings, Goswell Road, London EC1M 7BA; tel: 02072 518799; email: library@sog.org.uk; website: www.sog.org.uk.
Large range of books on various aspects of the textile industry with an online catalogue, which is searchable by subject as well as name.

The People's History Museum, Manchester.

Transcripts of parish registers, indexes to deposits in archives, indexes to wills, transcripts of some apprentices. Collections are listed under each county as well. Access to the library is free for members, otherwise there is a charge. A form of identification, for example, CARN ticket or driving licence, will be needed. For up-to-date details see their website.

• Trades Union Congress Library Collections, London Metropolitan University, Holloway Road Learning Centre, 236–250, Holloway Road, London N7 6PP; tel: 02071 332260; email: tuclib@londonmet.ac.uk; website: www.londonmet.ac.uk/services/sas/library-services/tuc/.
Books and documents relating to trade-union history.

• Working Class Movement Library, 51 The Crescent, Salford M5 4WX; tel: 01617 363601; email: enquiries@wcml.org.uk; website: www. wcml.org.uk/wcml/contact.htm.
Holds many trade-union records and publications, including membership records, minute books, journals and pamphlets, such as 'Our factory workers: the conditions under which they work', by C H Norman, published in 1907 by Twentieth Century Press. There are also some personal papers and biographies.

• British Library, India Office Records, 96 Euston Road, London NW1 2DB; tel: 02074 127873; email: oioc-enquiries@bl.uk; website: www.bl.uk/collections/orientalandindian.html.
The following websites give access to specific collections:

• Family history: www.bl.uk/collections/oiocfamilyhistory/family.
• Photographs: www.bl.uk/catalogues/indiaofficeselect/Photoform .asp.
• Prints, drawings and paintings: www.bl.uk/catalogues/indiaoffice select/PDForm.asp.
• Private papers, letters and diaries: www.bl.uk/catalogues/ indiaofficeselect/EMSForm.asp.
• Database of individuals: indiafamily.bl.uk/UI/Home.aspx.

All these are searchable.
  Published works about textiles and the textile industry are listed in the main printed book catalogue: catalogue.bl.uk.

12.2 Records in the East Midlands

• Birmingham University Information Services, Special Collections Department, Main Library, Edgbaston, Birmingham B15 2TT; tel: 01214 145838; email: special-collections@bham.ac.uk; website: www.special -coll.bham.ac.uk.
Holds records relating to John Westmacott & Co. (accounts records 1824–1838).

• Coventry Archives, Culture and Leisure, Community Services Directorate, Coventry City Council, Coventry Archives, John Sinclair House, Canal Basin, Coventry CV1 4LY; tel: 02476 785160; website: www.theherbert.org/collections/archives.
The Archives have a 'Guide to Business Records', which may be purchased by searchers. There is also a subject index that includes the various trades concerned (e.g., ribbon manufacturers) and persons and freemen's indexes, which will also identify people engaged therein.

• Derbyshire Record Office, New Street, Matlock DE4 3AG; correspondence address: County Hall, Matlock DE4 3AG; tel: 01629 58 0000, ext 59201; email: record.office@derbyshire.gov.uk; website: www.derbyshire.gov.uk/recordoffice.
Records for many textile businesses in the area, for example those of the Pares family, the Calver Mill Company, Longsden family and businesses, including family and business correspondence (late eighteenth century to the nineteenth century) between their companies set up in St Petersburg and later in South Carolina. Records of the Strutt family.

• Record Office for Leicester and Rutland, Long Street, Wigston Magna, Leicester LE18 2AH; tel: 01162 571080; email: recordoffice @leics.gov.uk; website: www.leics.gov.uk/index/community/museums/record_ office.htm.
Examples of records include those of the Hosiery and Allied Trades Research Association 1950–1987, bound volumes of *Leicestershire Trade Protection Society's Weekly Gazette of the Hosiery and Other Textiles Trades* 1901–1965.
Business records include: Atkins Brothers, Hosiery Manufacturers, Hinckley, Leicestershire (deeds and ledgers), Hanford and Miller, hosiers, Loughborough, Leicestershire 1838–1961 (miscellaneous papers but mostly from the twentieth century), Samuel Farmer and

Co., hosiery manufacturer, Leicester, which was taken over by Courtaulds in 1968 (some photographs and promotional leaflets), Raven and Co., hosiery manufacturers, Leicester 1884–1968 (financial records, stock records, insurance policies, various agreements and legal documents, welfare society 1887–1928, mostly minutes and financial but also new members, contributions book and pay-outs book), and W Preston and Son Ltd, manufacturer, Leicester 1877–1963, elastic web, manufacturers (company details and patents).

The records of T W Kempton Ltd, hosiery manufacturer, Leicester 1925–1977 include wages and salaries books, but there is a fifty year closure on these.

Records of J Lewin and Co., hosiery manufacturers, Wigston, Leicestershire 1805–1937 includes some very early wages books. Those of R and W H Symington and Co. Ltd, corset manufacturers, Market Harborough, Leicestershire 1776–1924 include a film archive and school-attendance certificates arranged in alphabetical order by surname, as well as some copies of birth certificates.

Benjamin Russell and Sons, Leicester, hosiery manufacturers 1825–1950 also have extensive records including business papers, wages books, age-certificate books 1842+, registers under the 1878 Act, registers under the 1901 Act, certificates of fitness under the 1902 Act, some personnel records, minutes of meetings and shares registers.

• Lincolnshire Archives, St Rumbold Street, Lincoln LN2 5AB; tel: for Search Room bookings 01522 782040, Search Room enquiries 01522 52 6204, Admin Office 01522 567137; email: enquiries – lincolnshire_ archive@lincolnshire.gov.uk, Search Room bookings – archive_ bookings@lincolnshire.gov.uk, Illustrations Index – Illustrations_Index @lincolnshire.gov.uk; website: www.lincolnshire.gov.uk/archives. Holds some records relating to flax and hemp bounty in the Lindsey area, but very little relating to textile industry.

• North East Lincolnshire Archives, Town Hall, Town Hall Square, Grimsby DN31 1HX; tel: 01472 323581; email: archives@nelincs.gov.uk. Contains Keadby Rope Manufacturers' letter book 1888–1894.

• Northamptonshire Record Office, Wootton Hall Park NN4 8BQ; tel: 01604 762129; email: archivist@northamptonshire.gov.uk; website: www.northamptonshire.gov.uk/Community/record/about_us.htm. Northamptonshire was not noted for large-scale textiles industries.

There was a substantial lace-making cottage industry but references to lace makers really only survive incidentally in the principal family history sources, such as parish registers and census returns. There are individual references in the subject index to various cloths and cloth sellers.

• Nottinghamshire Archives, County House, Castle Meadow Road, Nottingham NG2 1AG; tel: 01159 581634 (Search Room), 01159 504524 (Admin); website: www.nottinghamshire.gov.uk/archives.
The collections do not have extensive holdings on the textile industry, but records include: 'Memoirs' (typed copy) of Joseph Burdett, a stockinger of Lambley 1813–1817. 'Recollections' of J Moss, a stockinger of Lambley 1817. Diaries of Joseph Woolley of Clifton, frame knitter 1800–1815. Archives of Thomas Adams Co., lace manufacturers of Nottingham nineteenth to twentieth centuries, including a staff list for 1927. William Hollins and Co. Ltd, Hollins Mill, Pleasley Vale, Mansfield includes an incomplete list of shareholders 1917, but full list for 1931, wages books, rents book for houses at Pleasley Vale with address and name, some staff records.

In the Reference Library there is a card index by name, which also gives occupations of apprentices in Nottingham 1724–1882.

• University of Nottingham, King's Meadow Campus, Lenton Lane, Nottingham NG7 2NR; tel: 01159 514565; email: mss-library@ nottingham.ac.uk; website: www.nottingham.ac.uk/mss.
Records of George Brettle and Company Limited, hosiery manufacturers of Belper, Derbyshire, 1799–1984, comprising deeds, financial records, correspondence, staff-related records, including the Oberon Athletics Club as well as limited records for a number of other companies in the area. Contact the University for permission to view any of their collections.

• Glasgow University Archive Services, 13 Thurso Street, Glasgow G11 6PE; tel: 01413 305515; email: enquiries@archives.gla.ac.uk; website: www.archives.gla.ac.uk/service/all/searchrooms.html.
Although a Scottish Archive, it holds a range of records for various businesses, including Walter Evans & Co. Ltd (minute books 1905–1962, registers of members and share ledgers 1943–1963). Access subject to application to the University Archive department.

12.3 Records in Eastern England

• Bedfordshire and Luton Archives and Records Service, County Hall, Cauldwell Street, Bedford MK42 9AP; tel: 01234 228833; email: archive@bedscc.gov.uk; www.bedfordshire.gov.uk/archive.
Catalogues are currently being put online, including wills, deeds and Quarter Sessions records, etc. but few business records as such. The Bagshawe Collection contains some apprentice indentures. Records of Currant and Creak Ltd have a plan of the proposed factory, which was established during the 1920s. There are also details of former British Telecom properties and deposits from Marks & Spencer – many deeds also refer to those in textile trade.

• Cambridgeshire County Record Office, County Record Office, Box RES1009, Shire Hall, Cambridge CB3 0AP; tel: 01223 717281; website: www.cambridgeshire.gov.uk/leisure/archives.
Cambridgeshire has never had a large textile industry but the Consistory and Archdeaconry Courts of Ely Will indexes include a hundred individual weavers' wills, which may give family details.

• Essex Record Office, Wharf Road, Chelmsford CM2 6YT; tel: 01245 24 4644; email: ero.enquiry@essexcc.gov.uk; website: www.essexcc.gov. uk/ero.
The most important collections are the records of Courtaulds Ltd, silk weavers (ref D/F3), which include records of employees, and of Warners Ltd (ref D/F24), which include correspondence with the union about working conditions. The firm has reclaimed some of its archive to house in its own museum in Braintree and you should contact Warner Textile Archive, Warners Mill, Silks Way, Braintree CM7 3GB for access.

Other holdings include a microfilm of a diary of Joseph Buffon, weaver of Coggeshall 1677–1716 (ref: T/A156/1); petition of 1823 from weavers of Braintree, Bocking and Coggeshall against the repealing of an act regulating wages, which gives details of their wages (ref: D/DO/B50); and a manuscript autobiography of John Castle, silk weaver of Great Coggeshall 1819–1871 (ref: D/DU490/1).

SEAX is an electronic online catalogue available at: www.essexcc.gov.uk/ero. Select SEAX from the online service box, enter as a guest and then search using appropriate terms such as silk, weaving, weaver, etc.

• Hertfordshire Record Office, County Hall, Hertford SG13 8EJ; tel: 01438 737333; email: hertsdirect@hertscc.gov.uk; website: www.herts direct.org/heritage.
Records relating to silk mills and property transactions, but no personal details. Some material referring to the import of silk, cotton and other materials from abroad.

• Huntingdon County Record Office, Grammar School Walk, Huntingdon PE29 3LF; tel: 01480 375842; website: www.cambridgeshire .gov.uk/archives.
Huntingdonshire is not noted for textiles but holds the following records: Huntingdonshire hosiery mill plan *c.* 1924, costing book 1929–1931, order books 1930s–1950s, Eagley Cotton colour card 1962, *Hosiery Times* April 1960, file of papers, including notes on the history of the mill in the 1960s and photographs.

• Norfolk Record Office, The Archive Centre, Martineau Lane, Norwich NR1 2DQ; tel: 01603 222599; email: norfrec@norfolk.gov.uk.
Records of Gurney and other (mainly Stannard, Taylor and Taxtor) Norwich textile manufacturers 1751–1832. Grout and Co., Silk Textile Manufacturers, Great Yarmouth 1894–1974. *The Letters of Philip Stannard, Norwich Textile Manufacturer (1751–1763),* edited by Ursula Priestley, in Norfolk Record Society volume LVII (1992). Business records of tailors in Norwich, Thetford and Yarmouth and also records of the Norwich branch of the Amalgamated Society of Tailors 1880–1943 (SO108). Registers of freemen, apprentice indentures and other parish records include many references to weavers, spinners and other textile workers.

• Suffolk Record Office, Bury St Edmunds Branch, Raingate Street, Bury St Edmunds IP33 2AR; tel: 01284 352352; email: bury.ro @libher.suffolkcc.gov.uk; website: www.suffolkcc.gov.uk/sro/.
Apprentice indentures from the seventeenth and eighteenth centuries for weavers, spinners and wool combers. Glemsford Silk Mill plans and correspondence, later part of Anderson and Robertson Ltd, Glasgow. Messrs Ray, Oakes and Co., combers and yarn makers 1765/67. Plans, 1895–1923, for extension to silk mill, Gregory Street, for the Sudbury Silk Weaving Co. and Arnold & Gould Ltd, horsehair manufacturers.
• Suffolk Record Office, Ipswich Branch, Gatacre Road, Ipswich IP1

2LQ; tel: 01473 584541; email: ipswich.ro@libher.suffolkcc.gov.uk; website: www.suffolkcc.gov.uk/sro/.

Records of the Branwhite family of Lavenham, merchants, wool combers, clothiers 1731–1814, including individual items, such as bill headers, deeds, apprenticeship indentures as well as some wills and probate inventories and local newspapers. The *Ipswich Journal* newspaper has been indexed from 1800 to about 1840, on microfilm from the 1720s. Photographs and sale particulars for premises relating to the various textile trades. Library collection includes articles about aspects of the local textile trade.

• Suffolk Record Office, Lowestoft Branch, Lowestoft Record Office, Central Library, Clapham Road, Lowestoft, Suffolk NR32 1DR; tel: 01502 405357; website: www.suffolkcc.gov.uk/sro/.

Holds plans of buildings for the Artificial Silk Ltd sodium acetate factory for the twentieth century. Documents relating to individual weavers, mostly from the seventeenth and eighteenth centuries.

• Redbourn Village Museum, Silk Mill House, The Common, Redbourn AL3 7NB; tel: 01582 793397; email: redbournmuseum @aol.com; website: www.hertsmuseums.org.uk /info/redbourn.htm.

Certificates for children to work at the silk mill 1877–1879.

12.4 Records in the North East

Prior to 1974 this comprised the counties of Northumberland and Durham, but it is now divided into three areas: County Durham, Northumberland and Tyne & Wear, each having its own Record Office.

• Durham Record Office, County Hall, Durham DH1 5UL; tel: 01913 83 3253/3474; email: record.office@durham.gov.uk; website: www. durham.gov.uk/recordoffice.

Account book of the Woolcombers' Sick Association. Business and property records for Mackay's Carpet Factory, Durham. Some deeds for Henderson & Co., carpet manufacturers. Many apprenticeship records relating to the textile industry.

• Northumberland Collections Service, Queen Elizabeth II Country Park, Ashington NE63 9YF; tel: 01670 528035; email: LOSmith@ woodhorn.org.uk; website: www.experiencewoodhorn.com.

Records of the Morpeth Craft Guilds (sixteenth to nineteenth century), which included weavers, glovers, fullers and dyers. Society of Antiquaries of Newcastle upon Tyne collection refers to mercers. Records from Ashton Woollen Manufacturers based in Mitford, Northumberland.

• Tyne & Wear Archives Service, Blandford House, Blandford Square, Newcastle upon Tyne NE1 4JA; tel: 01912 326789; email: twas@ gateshead.gov.uk; website: www.tyneandweararchives.gov.uk.
Records of many guilds, such as tailors, weavers, upholsterers and Merchant Adventurers (incorporating drapers and mercers), curriers, felt makers, hatters, fullers and dyers, ropers, sail makers, weavers and Newcastle freemen. Gateshead guilds include: dyers, fullers, drapers, tailors and mercers. See User Guide 7 for further information. Business records include: Webster & Co. Ltd, rope makers of Sunderland and Joseph Crawhall & Sons Ltd, rope makers of Newcastle, records 1887–1962.

12.5 Records in the North West

All archives in the north west have some details relating to textile industries in their area.

• Bolton Archives and Local Studies Service, Central Library Civic Centre, Le Mans Crescent, Bolton BS1 1SE; tel: 01204 332185; email: archives.library@bolton.gov.uk; website: www.bolton.gov.uk.
There are a number of books and surveys relating to the cotton mills of Bolton from the 1700s. Papers relating to the Ainsworth family of Smithills Hall, bleachers and importers and exporters of cotton cloth. Union records of a number of different unions. Personal reminiscences by cotton workers in Bolton.

• Bury Archives Service, Moss Street, Bury BL9 0DG; tel: 01612 536782; email: archives@bury.gov.uk; website: www.bury.gov.uk/archives.
Business records for many of the firms in the area, apprentice indentures and union records for local branches.

• Cheshire Record Office, Duke Street, Chester CH1 1RL; tel: 01244 60 2574; email: recordoffice@cheshire.gov.uk; website: www.cheshire. gov.uk/recordoffice.htm.

Some small collections of business records, including Josiah Smale and Son Ltd 1772–1964, Swindells of Bollington 1804–1915, Brocklehurst Fabrics Ltd, silk weavers and printers 1756–1970 (administrative and design records). Records of trade associations: South and East Cheshire Textile Association 1909–1994.

• Cumbria Record Office, The Castle, Carlisle CA3 8UR; tel: 01228 60 7285; email:carlisle.record.office@cumbriacc.gov.uk; website: www. cumbria.gov.uk/archives.
Business records include those of R R Buck of Carlisle 1848–1967, Coward, Philipson & Co., bobbin manufacturers of Keswick 1867–1959, Cumberland Mills, Warwick Bridge 1916, Ferguson Brothers of Carlisle 1830–1979, Morton Sundour of Carlisle 1911–1914 and Stead McAlpin of Cummersdale 1885–1943.

• Greater Manchester County Record Office, 56 Marshall Street, New Cross, Manchester M4 5FU; tel: 01618 325284; email: archives @gmcro.co.uk; website: www.gmcro.co.uk.
Records relating to businesses in the area, including some company records relating to the Strutt family and the Tootal Group. There is a thirty year closure on these documents and the majority relate to the running of the company, meetings, shareholders and directors, though there are some employee and pension records too. Other holdings include volumes of the *Journal of the Textile Industry*, records of Textile Employers' Associations, records of various businesses, including Courtaulds and some of its subsidiaries, records of a number of trade unions and associations.

• Lancashire Record Office, Bow Lane, Preston PR1 2RE; tel: 01772 53 3039; email: record.office@ed.lancscc.gov.uk; website: www.archives .lancashire.gov.uk.
There are many archives of textile firms in Lancashire and a range of union records and employers' associations. Family papers, including those of the Horrocks family of Preston and a fair amount of biographical material. Very large and detailed archive of Platt Saco Lowell (formerly Platts), which made machinery for textile mills (DDPSL).

• Lancaster University Library, Bailrigg, Lancaster LA1 4YH; tel: 01524 592516; email: library@lancs.ac.uk; website: libweb.lancs.ac.uk.

No business records or personal papers but the Lancashire Textile Project comprises a series of interviews with people concerned with all aspects of the Lancashire textile industry, including its technology and its links with the local communities. Includes tapes, cassette copies, transcripts and associated photographs.

The Pasold Research Fund's library is currently held at Lancaster. The Fund's field of interest covers the history of textiles generally.

• Liverpool Record Office and Local History Service, City Libraries, William Brown Street, Liverpool L3 8EW; tel: 01512 335817; email: recoffice.central.library@liverpool.gov.uk; website: www.liverpool. gov.uk.
Records principally relate to the cotton industry, including the records of the Cotton Association, which grew out of cotton trading between merchants and brokers, being established in 1882 to provide regulation and arbitration for the cotton industry.

Local history section relating to the cotton industry and the cotton trade, including books, periodical and newspaper articles, newspaper cuttings and photographs.

• Manchester Archives and Local Studies, Central Library, St Peter's Square, Manchester M2 5PD; tel: 01612 341980; email: archiveslocal studies@manchester.gov.uk; website: www.manchester.gov.uk/ libraries/arls/.
Extensive collection relating to the local cotton industry, including, e.g., records of the National Association of Powerloom Overlookers 1871–1984, J and N Philips and Co. Ltd of Tean, Staffordshire, and of Manchester, Manufacturers and Textiles, Tapes and Smallwares 1748–1968, R Greg and Co. Ltd of Quarry Bank Mill, Styal 1771–1952, W G and J Strutt Ltd of Belper, Derbyshire, cotton spinners 1771–1936, papers of John Bury, Calico Printer 1764–1972.

• Oldham Local Studies and Archives, 84 Union Street, Oldham OL1 1DN; tel: 01617 704654; email: archives@oldham.gov.uk; website: www.oldham.gov.uk/community/local_studies/oldhams-archives.htm.
Extensive collection relating to the local cotton industry, including, for example, the Oldham Operative Cotton Spinners 1845–1972, Oldham Provincial Union of Textile and Allied Workers 1866–1981, Highams Limited 1848–1989, Oldham Operative Cotton Spinners 1845–1972 and Oldham and Rochdale Textile Employers' Association 1866–2000.

• Local Studies Centre, Touchstones, Rochdale, The Esplanade, Rochdale Lancs OL16 1AQ; tel: 01706 924915; email: localstudies @rochdale.gov.uk.
Mainly background information but also holds details of the English Sewing Cotton Company's mills (Bridgewater Mills), Pendlebury. Some of the material is in a poor condition and access to it may be restricted.

• Information Services Division, University of Salford, Salford M5 4WT; tel: 01612 956650; website: www.isd.salford.ac.uk/library/ resources/special/.
Records include the English Velvet and Cord Dyers' Association incorporated 1899, amalgamating fourteen firms engaged in the cotton-velvet and corduroy dyeing industry. The company went out of business in 1950s; its last name was E V Industrials Ltd. The records mostly consist of minute books and deeds.

• Stockport Central Library, Wellington Road South, Stockport SK1 3RS; tel: 01614 744530; email: localheritagelibrary@stockport.gov.uk; website: www.stockport.gov.uk/content/leisureculture/libraries/ localheritagelibrary.
Details of Greg's mill, Reddish, and the Portwood Spinning Company are the main collections, but these do not give names and addresses of employees.

• Tameside Local Studies and Archives Centre, Tameside Central Library, Old Street, Ashton-under-Lyne OL6 7SG; tel: 01613 424242; email: localstudies.library@tameside.gov.uk; website: www.tameside. gov.uk/history.
Two oral-history collections from Tameside recorded from c. 1976 to recent times, which include a lot of mill workers and a special sub-collection of mill workers in Hyde, recorded by the Living Memories of Hyde Project. Also, Manchester Studies tapes, which include mill workers from all over the north west. Also, there are many trade-union records and some business records.

• Wigan Archives Service, Town Hall, Market Square, Leigh WN7 2DY; tel: 01942 404431; email: heritage@wict.gov.uk; website: www.wict.org /Culture/Heritage/archives.htm.

Apprentice records, many relating to children sent to mills. Earlier ones are often to linen weavers. Also, records of J and J Hayes, which later became part of Courtaulds, Pennington Mill Company Ltd – some records are fairly recent and may be restricted – and Fine Cotton Spinners' and Doublers' Association Ltd, Lancashire.

• Wirral Archives Service, Wirral Museum, Town Hall, Hamilton Square, Birkenhead, Wirral CH41 5BR; tel: 01516 663903; website: www.wirral-libraries.net/archives.
No extensive textile records held, but does include those of Ellis and Co. (wages books 1880–1913, time books 1909–1926, photographs (including unnamed staff at work)), and Gandy Ltd (photograph of office staff 1912).

12.6 Records in the South East

• Berkshire Record Office, 9 Coley Ave, Reading RG1 6AF; tel: 0118 901 5132; email: ARCH@Reading.gov.uk; website: www.berkshirerecord office.org.uk.
This has card indexes for cloth, clothiers and cloth workers; wool, weaving, spinning, mills; business records; indenture records; wages records for the various industries; street directories; biographies. There are also deeds and other documents that often give details of occupations relating to textile industry.

• Centre for Buckinghamshire Studies, County Hall, Walton Street, Aylesbury HP20 1UU; tel: 01296 382587; email: archives@buckscc .gov.uk; website: www.buckscc.gov.uk/archives.
Records of the local area, including those of Samuel Very 1684–1701, hemp dresser, of Wendover, Buckinghamshire (business correspondence); Carrington family/Barons Carrington (deeds of co-partnership 1765–1791, references to flax, hemp and yarn trades); sale particulars of Tring Park, including Tring Silk Mill 1872; Waddesdon; Messuage, formerly a beerhouse converted in 1854 into a silk mill or factory 1849; printed list of subscribers to fund for establishing the Aylesbury Straw Plait Society with statement of accounts 1846; and Charles Featherstonhaugh of Woburn Sands, rope manufacturer (deeds).

• Centre for Kentish Studies, Sessions House, County Hall, Maidstone, Kent ME14 1XQ; tel: 01622 694363; email: archives@kent.gov.uk;

website: www.kentarchives.org.
The centre has indexes that can be searched for information, including subject indexes under trades, industry and business, and also a personal-names index. Records of flax bounties *c.* 1793–1800, wills and inventories for the dioceses of Rochester and Canterbury, as well as deeds and apprentice indentures. There are 'Guides' to the contents of the centre and specialised publications on relevant subjects.

• East Sussex Record Office, The Maltings, Castle Precincts, Lewes BN7 1YT; tel: 01273 482349; email: archives@eastsussex.gov.uk; website: www.eastsussex.gov.uk/useourarchives.
There is a register of hemp and flax bounties 1783–1795, as well as local businesses such as wool merchants Brazier and Sons (later Messrs Legg), Rye (correspondence and accounts 1820s–1900).

• Hampshire Record Office, Sussex Street, Winchester SO23 8TH; tel: 01962 846154; email: enquiries.archives@hants.gov.uk; website: www.hants.gov.uk/record-office.
There is an excellent online database at www.hants.gov.uk/record-office/catalog/index.html, which can be used to find individuals who may have been involved in the textile industry.

• Isle of Wight Record Office, 26 Hillside, Newport PO30 2EB; tel: 019 83 823820/1; email: record.office@iow.gov.uk; website: www.iwight. com/library/record_office.
There is a newspaper article about the history of Nunn's Lace Factory, the information about which was supplied by a former machinist and designer at the factory, Henry Shephard. Carisbrooke Castle Museum has some examples of lace made at the factory in its collections.

• Oxfordshire Record Office, St Luke's Church, Temple Road, Cowley, Oxford OX4 2HT; tel: 01865 398200; email: archives@oxfordshire .gov.uk; website: www.oxfordshire.gov.uk/records.
Textile industries include the Early Blanket Company records at Witney 1711–1992, which contain weaving, dyeing, spinning, financial records, also some genealogical information about the family; tailors such as Shepherd & Woodward Tailor, Gents Outfitter 1907–1981, which includes some records of James Clarke & Son Robemakers 1849–1963; Arbery & Son of Wantage 1890–1993, haberdashers; Costell & Son Tailors and Robemakers, Oxford; Zacharias & Co., waterproof

clothing manufacturers 1933–1965 and deeds and leases relating to the Collier family, blanket manufacturers. Records of organisations such as the Witney Blanket Weavers' Company, incorporated by Royal Charter in 1711; wills, which include those of many blanket weavers, fullers, tuckers and other blanket-related occupations; poor-law papers, including apprenticeship indentures. There is a subject-index card system.

• West Sussex Record Office, County Hall, Chichester PO19 1RN; tel: 01243 753600; email: records.office@westsussex.gov.uk; website: www.westsussex.gov.uk/ro/.
Though there was very little textile production in West Sussex after about 1700, Chichester was an important centre for the manufacture of woollen cloth in the sixteenth century. A Guild for Clothworkers and Dyers was established in 1616. The indenture establishing the Guild is at City of Chichester (WSRO City of Chichester AH/11); also available online. There is a card index by surname to Chichester tradesmen in the seventeenth century, and this includes a section on clothiers. The records of the Office of Ulnager of Cloth for Surrey and Sussex are included among the Loseley Mss and these are held at the Surrey History Centre, 130 Goldsworth Road, Woking GU21 6ND; tel: 01483 518737.

• Bexley Local Studies and Archive Centre, Central Library, Townley Road, Bexleyheath DA6 7HJ; tel: 02088 367369; email: archives @bexley.gov.uk; website: www.bexley.gov.uk.
There are a number of building plans for various silk mills.

• Templeman Library, University of Kent at Canterbury, Special Collections, The CP Davies Collection of Mill Memorabilia, Canterbury, Kent CT2 7NU; website: library.kent.ac.uk/ library/.

• National Maritime Museum, Park Row, Greenwich, London SE10 9NF; tel: 02083 126750; email: manuscripts@nmm.ac.uk; website: www.nmm.ac.uk.
Records include those of Ratsey & Lapthorn Ltd, sail and flag makers 1825–36, 1887–92 (account and order book and letter book).

• Gosport Discovery Centre, High Street, Gosport, Hampshire PO12 1BT; tel: 08456 035631; website: www3.hants.gov.uk/gdc.

12.7 Records in London

• Bromley Local Studies & Archives, Central Library, High Street, Bromley BR1 1EX; tel: 02084 617170; email: localstudies.library @bromley.gov.uk; website: www.library.bromley. gov.uk /archive.
On the webpage is a link to the archives catalogue: www.library .bromley.gov.uk/archive/index.htm.
There are few resources to do with textiles in the Bromley area but the existence of calico printing on the River Darenth is reflected in settlement examinations taken before magistrates of the Bromley division in the later eighteenth to early nineteenth centuries (ref.613/1-3). The examinations have been indexed by volunteers and can be searched by surname.

• Hammersmith and Fulham Archives and Local History Centre, The Lilla Huset, 191 Talgarth Road, London W6 8BJ; tel: 02087 415159; email: archives@lbhf.gov.uk; website: www.lbhf.gov.uk.
Very little held relating to the textile industry except the apprenticeship indenture of Elizabeth Druce, aged 10 years, poor child of Hammersmith, bound to David Ainsworth of Blackbarrow, parish of Colton, Lancashire, cotton manufacturer, 28 March 1810, and the papers of Annie Woolger (1899–1992), dressmaker of Fulham, including fashion sketches, albums, correspondence, photographs, embroidery samples (includes some done by her grandmother) c. 1852–c. 1990.

• Haringey Archive Service, Bruce Castle Museum, Lordship Lane, Tottenham, London N17 8NU; tel: 02088 088772; email: museum.services@haringey.gov.uk; website: www.haringey. gov.uk/ index/community_and_leisure/time_out_in_haringey/visiting_ haringey/places_to_visit/brucecastlemuseum/archives.htm.
Very little on the textile industry except accounts of Edmonds Denham & Goyder Ltd, drapers of Wood Green, which was formed by the amalgamation of Edmonds Brothers and Denham & Goyder.

• Guildhall Library, City of London, Aldermanbury EC2P 7HH. Manuscripts – tel: 02073 321862/02073 321863, 02073 323803 (Textphone); email: manuscripts.guildhall@cityoflondon.gov.uk. Printed books – tel 02073 321868/02073 321870, 02073 323803 (Textphone); email: printedbooks.guildhall@cityoflondon.gov.uk.

Website: www.cityoflondon.gov.uk/Corporation/leisure_heritage/ libraries_archives_museums_galleries/city_london_libraries/guildhal l_lib.htm.

The Guildhall Library in London is an important resource for investigating textile ancestry around the London area and beyond. It is a public library so an appointment is not necessary.

The library has an extensive collection of books relating to general business history. Bibliographies give details of any firms for which there is a published history, together with details of where their archives may be found. Anyone who held a high position in a large company can probably be traced through directories or dictionaries, such as the Directory of Directors.

Company registrations (microfilm index) from 1856–1973 can be useful for looking up the registration number and date of incorporation, but printed sources are available as well.

The records of a very large number of businesses that were based in the City of London are held here, including companies directly

The Guildhall, London.

involved in the industry, ranging from large organisations like Anglo-Russian Cotton Factories and Ede and Ravenscroft Ltd to small firms of merchants and traders, for example, Richard Archedale, a seventeenth-century draper, or Major Blundell, an eighteenth-century haberdasher.

Bankruptcies, dissolutions and liquidations

There are a number of indexes relating to company dissolutions available on microfiche and printed indexes to notices of bankruptcies from the *London Gazette*. The Register of Defunct Companies and *Perry's Gazette* may contain references to textile companies.

Annual reports

There are annual reports from companies that were listed on the London Stock Exchange for the years 1880–1965. First check Stock Exchange Official Intelligence 1882–1933 to see if the company was listed. Make a note of which industry and the company category or sub-category, such as Textiles – Clothing, Cotton and Synthetics, Wool, and Miscellaneous Textiles. Reports are filed alphabetically within categories. You will need to give advance notice if you wish to use these reports as they are not kept at the library.

Other company information such as prospectuses (1824–1964) are also available, but applications for listing Shares on the Stock Exchange 1850–1988 are held in the Manuscript Section where there is a card index.

Newspapers

- *The Times* 1785 onwards (microfilm) – printed index from 1790.
- *Financial Times* 1888 onward (microfilm) – printed index from 1981.
- *The Times* Digital Archive 1785–1985.

Other business magazines are also held but these are general, not specific to the textile industry.

Directories

London directories from 1677 onwards and national directories from 1781 onwards.

Apprenticeship records

• Index (microfiche) to some apprenticeships 1710–1774.
• Published lists and indexes for some apprentices in other towns, such as Oxford (1697–1800) and Coventry (1781–1806).
• Records to many of the City of London Livery Companies (Guilds) (see Chapter 1).

Brief details of all the livery company records available in the Library are given in *City Livery Companies and related organisations: a guide to their archives in Guildhall Library*. Details of surviving membership records held by the library are given in *Livery Company Membership Guide*, available on the Manuscripts Section's website at: www.history.ac.uk /gh/livintro.htm. The website www.history.ac.uk/gh/livlist.htm lists all companies of London with details of where the records are held if they exist, whether there are any indexes to the records, the dates of the records and brief details of what they are, such as freedom registers, apprentice-binding books etc. The Framework Knitters records include some freemen admitted from the Midlands area.

   To find out which company an ancestor may have belonged to, check the trade directories for details of their occupation. In the Printed Books Section of Guildhall Library is the supplement to the Universal British Directory of 1793, 1796 and 1798 in which is a list, dated 1792, of liverymen of the City of London, with their livery company.

Merchant Taylors' Company

• Apprentices 1398–1557 – see the wardens' accounts (Ms 34048/1-4), which are not indexed. Only a few of these have survived.

• Apprentices 1486–93 – the surviving Court minutes (Ms 34008/1-2) have been transcribed and indexed by Matthew Davies, *The Merchant Taylors' Company of London: Court Minutes, 1486–93* (2000).

• Apprentices 1562–1583 – see the minutes of 'Ordinary Courts' (in Ms 34010/1-2), not indexed. After this date it is better to consult the apprentice-bindings books (Ms 34038/1-21). These also contain details of any apprentices who were transferred or 'turned over' to new masters.

• Apprentices 1583–1933 – see the registers of apprentice bindings 1583–1933 (Ms 34038/1-21).

• The orphan-tax books 1694–1861 (Ms 34041/1-3) record names of apprentices bound between these dates, but very little detail is given.

• Freemen 1398–1493 – see the modern indexes (Ms 34033) and associated biographical notes (Ms 34034), which are based upon the early wardens' account books 1398–1484 (gaps) (Ms 34048/1-3) and the fragmentary Court minutes for 1486–1493 (Ms 34008/1-2).

• Freemen 1493–1530 – no surviving sources.

• Freemen 1530–1928 – see Ms 34037/1-4, index of freemen 1530–1928 which is in alphabetical order.

• Freemen 1562 onwards – see the 'Ordinary Court' minutes for 1562–1595 (Ms 34010/1-2), 1595–1648 (Ms 34017/1-5) and 1648 to twentieth century (Ms 34018/3-10).

• Livery 1398–1493 – see the modern indexes (Ms 34033) and associated biographical notes (Ms 34034). These are based upon the early wardens' account books 1398–1484 (gaps) (Ms 34048/1-3) and the fragmentary Court minutes for 1486–1493 (Ms 34008/1-2).

• Livery and Court 1530–1928 – there was a small number of freemen who were admitted to the livery or subsequently to the Court. They are indicated in the index of freemen 1530–1928 (Ms 34037/1-4), which gives the date of admission to the livery. Livery admissions can be found in the minutes of both full and 'Ordinary' Courts (Ms 34010, 34017-8), while various livery and Court lists survive from the late seventeenth century (Mss 34024-31).

Fire-insurance records

Mainly London-based fire-insurance company records, but these often insured buildings in the regions and quickly established agents in many parts of the country. The earliest records include:

• The Hand-in-Hand Fire and Life Insurance Society (1696) – most policies have name indexes and some numerical and topographical indexes.

• The Sun Insurance Office (established as the Sun Fire office in 1710) – mostly unindexed.

• The Royal Exchange Assurance (established in 1720) – mostly unindexed.

Some published card or microfiche indexes to some policy registers are available in the Library but there is also a searchable online index to Sun policy registers Ms 11936/471-500, dating from 1816–1838 available at www.nationalarchives.gov.uk/a2a. This is an ongoing project and further records will be added in the future.

• London Metropolitan Archives, 40 Northampton Road, Clerkenwell, London EC1R 0HB; website: www.cityoflondon.gov.uk/Corporation/leisure_heritage/libraries_archives_museums_galleries/lma/.
Few records that relate to the textile business specifically, but some mention in deeds and other documents that refer to silk merchants or other silk workers, calico printers, dyers and so on.

Property records such as an assignment (Business Transaction) for Matthew Ferris of Longford, calico printer, and Henry Francis Smith of Coleman Street, City of London, wool broker, dated 1829.

Memorandum of proclamation prohibiting the making or wearing of demicasters or using wool with beaver in beaver hats, dated 1639.

Petitions to Justices for regulations of wages in the silk industry 1770–1825.

Apprenticeship indentures for some pauper apprentices who went to northern mills.

Deed of covenant and indemnity for apprentices at the Flax Mills at Hounslow. The schedule has names of apprentices, age at which apprenticed and their origin 1821.

• City of Westminster Archives, 10 St Ann's Street, London SW1P 2DE; tel: 02076 415180; email: archives@westminster.gov.uk; website: www.westminster.gov.uk/archives.
This has a variety of magazines and booklets relating to the textile industry generally. There is an online catalogue on their website. Records include those for Holland and Sherry, woollen fabric merchants, Savile Row, 1844–1917, including details of creditors and debtors, staff records and partnership agreements. The Tilbury papers relate to a warehousing business, but include many bills for clients, some of whom were in the textile trade. Some apprenticeship indentures are held. There are a number of archive-centre guides which give further details of collections held.

• Tower Hamlets Local History Library and Archives, Bancroft Library, 277 Bancroft Road, London E1 4DQ; tel: 02073 641290; email: localhistory@towerhamlets.gov.uk; website: www.ideastore.co.uk/.
Hawkins & Tipson Ltd, rope makers, Isle of Dogs: records 1882–1948.

12.8 Records in the South West

• Bristol Record Office, 'B' Bond Warehouse, Smeaton Road, Bristol BS1 6XN; tel: 01179 224224; email: bro@bristol.gov.uk; website: www.bristol.gov.uk.
An online catalogue is available at: www.archives.bristol-city.gov.uk.

Records include apprentice records, from 1532, including clothier, shearman, tucker, weaver, as well as cappers and tailors, giving name and place of residence of the apprentice's father, often from quite a distance, for example, a boy from Kendal apprenticed in 1595 to a Bristol dyer. Many apprentices went on to become free of the city and are recorded in the burgess books. There are probate inventories (1542–1804), which can list a craftsman's tools of the trade or stock in the shop and some wills. Some records of the Great Western Cotton Factory, including sample of cloth made in the factory. Some of the weavers came from Lancashire. Church records for some rural parishes adjoining Bristol, including Westerleigh and Frampton Cotterell, which were hatting/felt-making areas. Settlement papers and examinations often contain reference to apprenticeship to a felt maker, narrow weaver, hatter etc. There is a personal-names index to the settlement papers.

• Cornwall Record Office, Old County Hall , Truro TR1 3AY; tel: 01872 323127; email: CRO@cornwall.gov.uk; website: www.cornwall.gov.uk.
Records mainly relate to family drapers or rope manufacturers and the individual collections can be found via the National Register of Archives.

• Devon Record Office, Great Moor House, Bittern Road, Sowton, Exeter EX2 7NL; tel: 01392 384253; email: devrec@devon.gov.uk; website: www.devon.gov.uk/record.office.htm.
Extensive records of Heathcoat of Tiverton, lace manufacturers. Company of Weavers, Tuckers and Shearmen of Exeter, which contains minutes and other records from 1565. There is a subject card index with a number of references to the textile trades and this can be consulted by anybody visiting the office.

The book *Exeter Freemen, 1266–1967,* edited by Margery Rowe and Andrew Jackson (Devon and Cornwall Record Society, Extra Series I, 1973), can be found here.

• Dorset History Centre, Bridport Road, Dorchester DT1 1RP; tel: 01305 250550; email: archives@dorsetcc.gov.uk; website: www.dorsetforyou .com/archives.
Records include Thomas Tucker & Co. Ltd, net, cordage and canvas manufacturers 1782–1918 (cash books, ledgers, outbraiders' book); 1807–1851 (miscellaneous correspondence and accounts). Pymore Mill Co. Ltd, twine and thread manufacturers 1842–1851 (register and sales accounts); 1843–61 (building specifications and papers). There are also apprenticeship indentures, some of which relate to the rope and twine industry.

• Gloucestershire Archives, Clarence Row, Alvin Street, Gloucester GL1 3DW; tel: 01452 425295; email: archives@gloucestershire.gov.uk; website: www.gloucestershire.gov.uk/archives.
Wills, gaol registers, local reference books on historical and genealogical subjects, as well as comprehensive indexes (compiled from the catalogues in the Record Office) that cover personal names, place names and subjects, as well as a prints and photographic index.

Business records include those of Winterbotham, Strachan & Playne, cloth manufacturers, Longford and Cam (correspondence, plans and technical reports 1913–1988); William Playne and Co. Ltd, Minchinhampton, woollen manufacturers; Kemp and Hewitt, Trowbridge, Wiltshire, woollen manufacturers; Hunt & Winterbottom 1817–1962 (minutes, share, financial and stock records, wool, weavers, spinners and pattern books, plans and valuations). There are also applications for flax bounty (1795). The roll for 1756 has an important petition from weavers and counter-petition from the clothiers, concerning a wage dispute. Another useful source of information on the cloth and textile industry can be found on the Digital Stroud website: www.digitalstroud.co.uk.

• North Devon Record Office, Tuly Street, Barnstaple EX31 1EL; tel: 01271 388608; email: ndevrec@devon.gov.uk; website: www.devon.gov. uk/record_office.htm.
The wool industry was important to Barnstaple, and sources found in the records of the borough (ref B1) reflect this. A machine-lace factory

was established in the nineteenth century and there are scattered records of the families employed there (brought together in a recent book by Peter Christie and Deborah Gahan, *Barnstaple's Vanished Lace Industry*, Lazarus Press, 1998). Records include those of the Staple Vale woollen manufactory, Torrington 1777–1885 and Reed, woolstaplers of Torrington nineteenth to twentieth century

• Somerset Archive and Record Service, Somerset Record Office, Obridge Road, Taunton TA2 7PU; tel: 01823 337600 (Appointments), 01823 278805 (Enquiries); email: archives@somerset.gov.uk; website: www.somerset.gov.uk/archives.
The majority of the catalogues, including the catalogue to the Quarter Sessions papers, can be viewed online.

Records include papers relating to the Parsons family of Martock and the manufacture of sailcloth, webbing and other textiles in Somerset (and Dorset) 1797–1988; business records of Clark, Son and Morland, sheepskin-glove and glove manufacturers, Street and Glastonbury 1893–1970. Other records include deeds (often found among estate collections, solicitors' collections and private collections), apprenticeship indentures, settlement examinations, Quarter Sessions papers and wills. Some indexes available in the search room. There are card indexes to wills but the majority of the wills for Somerset were destroyed during the Second Word War.

• Wiltshire and Swindon Record Office, Cocklebury Road, Chippenham SN15 3QN; tel: 01249 705500; email: wsro@wiltshire .gov.uk; website: www.wiltshire.gov.uk/history-centre.htm.
There are various books on the woollen trade published by Ken Rogers, a local historian. Also business records of Samuel Salter, J & T Clarke and Palmer Mackay – all Trowbridge companies. Wilton Carpet Factory, including pattern books, wool samples and in some cases photographs of the factories themselves. A Laverton & Co. worsted manufacturer 1805–1968 (financial records, stock book, order and pattern books, valuation and photographs). Charles Case & Sons, tanners 1890–1983 (letter books, correspondence, financial records, costing and stock books, wages records). Wilkins & Darking, clothiers 1930–1985 (minutes, accounts and correspondence). C W Maggs & Co. (Melksham) Ltd, rope and matting manufacturers 1899–1969 (financial records, shipping ledger). A L Jefferies (Glover) 1922–1974 (minutes, register of members – see The National Archives for access details).

• Stroudwater Textile Trust, c/o Ian Mackintosh, 6 Castle Villas, Stroud, Gloucestershire GL5 2HP; email: imack@btopenworld.com.
The Stroudwater Textile Trust is a small voluntary organisation and has a limited number of records about some clothier families and also some nineteenth-century records from William Playne & Co. of Longfords Mill. It has no resources for visitors to research and can only respond to a limited number of enquiries. Demonstrations of machinery can be seen at various local mills during the summer months.

12.9 Records in Wales

• Carmarthenshire Archive Service, Parc Myrddin Richmond Terrace, Carmarthen SA31 1DS; tel: 01267 228232; email: archives@ carmarthenshire.gov.uk; website: www.carmarthenshire.gov.uk/eng.
Some records of Bargod Woollen Mills, Dre-fach Felindre, mainly advertisements but also the memorandum of agreement 1889 and correspondence 1881–1920; there are notes on the Welsh woollen industry with illustrative documents and photographs of the Mill 1975. The records of Jones Bros, woollen manufacturers *c*. 1901–1906 include a register of employees at Ryhdwyrm Woollen Mill (pronounced ridworm). Those of John Jones, woollen manufacturers, Drefach *c*. 1880–1921 include correspondence, vouchers and miscellaneous papers.

• Ceredigion Archives, Swyddfa'r Sir, Marine Terrace, Aberystwyth SY23 2DE; tel: 01970 633697/8; email: archives@ceredigion.gov.uk; website: archifdy-ceredigion.org.uk/.
Records of the Cilcennin Woollen Factory and a collection that contains (among other items) several CDs with scanned images of Lerry Tweed Mills in Talybont from the 1930s to the present day. This mill was run as a family business until the 1980s. There were very many small textile mills in Cardiganshire – contact Royal Commission on the Ancient and Historical Monuments of Wales, Library and Reader Services, National Monuments Record of Wales, Plas Crug, Aberystwyth SY23 1NJ; tel: 01970 621200 or The Welsh Mills Society, The Secretary, Y Felin, Tynygraig, Ystrad Meurig, Ceredigion SY25 6AE.

• Denbighshire Record Office, 46 Clwyd Street, Ruthin LL15 1HP; tel: 01824 708250; email: archives@denbighshire.gov.uk; website: www. denbighshire.gov.uk.

Excellent subject index, which is available on the Denbighshire website at http:www.denbighshire.gov.uk/archives. Examples from this include a partnership agreement of Sykes, Allen and Co., cotton brokers of Liverpool 1888, extracts from the memoirs of John Hughes, woollen manufacturer, Llangollen 1810–1840, Welsh woollen industry (official list of manufacturers 1960s), William Jones & Son, Llangollen Mill 1971–1973 (delivery books).

• Flintshire Record Office, The Old Rectory, Rectory Lane, Hawarden CH5 3NR; tel: 01244 532364; email: archives@flintshire.gov.uk; website: www.flintshire.gov.uk/archives.
Records relating to Courtaulds in Flintshire.

• Glamorgan Record Office, Glamorgan Building, King Edward VII Avenue, Cathays Park, Cardiff CF10 3NE; tel: 02920 780282; email: glamro@cardiff.ac.uk; website: www.glamro.gov.uk.
Records relating to Pandy woollen mill, Caerphilly, including William Austin's accounts book for spinning 1858–1859, an article 'The woollen industry of Caerphilly' by Glyndwr G Jones 1957, with samples of cloth and two cloth accounts books 1858–1861 and 1872–1873.

• Gwynedd Archives, Caernarfon Record Office, Victoria Dock, Caernarfon LL55 1SH; tel: 01286 679095/9088.
Account book of Penmachno Woollen Mill 1849–1872 and a pamphlet on the Bryncir Woollen Mill.

• National Library of Wales: Department of Collection Services, Aberystwyth SY23 3BU; tel: 01970 632800; email: holi@llgc.org.uk; website: www.llgc.org.uk. Family history section website: www.llgc .org.uk/ht/index_s.htm.
Example records include those of the Welshpool Woollen Co. 1843–1852 (minutes and accounts), and Jones & Morris, sail makers 1888–1920 (with W Morris & Co.), Llanidloes Welsh Flannel Tweed & Wool Stapling Co. c. 1860 (correspondence, accounts and legal papers), Welsh Woollen Manufacturers Association 1954–1961 (records). The library also holds the Welsh Probate Records.

• Archives Department, University of Wales Bangor, College Road, Bangor LL57 2DG; tel: 01248 382966 or 01248 383276; email: iss177 @bangor.ac.uk; website: www.bangor.ac.uk/is/library/ special.html.

Meyrick Family Linen and Woollen Industries Transcript, an important document from the point of view of domestic industries in the eighteenth century, the rope and mat makers of Newborough and the relationship between Anglesey and Irish merchants.

Records of the Ceiriog Valley Woollen Mills (ledgers, wool books, cash books, sales books, order books, weaving books and wages records). Ledgers show names of companies with which the mill traded, prices of wool, flannel and transport costs. Wool books include consignment details with date of purchase, quality, weight and amount of foreign wool.

12.10 Records in Yorkshire

Archives in Yorkshire, particularly in West Yorkshire, have extensive records relating to the textile industry of their area.

• Barnsley Archive and Local Studies Department, Central Library, Shambles Street, Barnsley S70 2JF; tel: 01226 773950; email: Archives@barnsley.gov.uk; website: www.barnsley.gov.uk/bguk/Leisure_Culture/Libraries.
Deeds and leases etc., which often refer to textile workers, e.g., Foljambe Wood of Ackworth, in the county of York, linen manufacturer, bankrupt 1796; Thomas Winsmore Wilson of Barnsley, in the County of York, linen manufacturer 1834; Thomas Taylor of Dodworth, in the parish of Silkstone, in the county of York, linen manufacturer. Taylor's Linen Mill, Peel Street, Barnsley, records include a cassette of oral-history interviews with former linen-mill workers at Borespring Mill, Barnsley, and Redbrook Mill, Barnsley. Also accompanying notes and illustrations May 1992. There are photographs showing Taylor's Linen Mill, Barnsley, and Midland and Smithies Bleachworks, Barnsley.

• Doncaster Archives, King Edward Road, Doncaster DN4 0NA; tel: 01302 859811; email: doncaster.archives@doncaster.gov.uk; website: www.doncaster.gov.uk/doncasterarchives.
There are general subject and personal-name card indexes. Occasionally there are references to members of the Guild of Weavers, Walkers and Shearmen in the records of the corporation from the sixteenth century onwards. Doncaster Township Overseers of the Poor memorandum book of the overseers 1794–1795 includes references to

children made pauper apprentices at the cotton mill of Davison and Hawksley, Arnold, Nottinghamshire. The Bridon Plc (formerly British Rope Ltd) archive has extensive, but few personnel, records. Access to these records is restricted to those with prior permission from Bridon Plc. Intending users should first contact the Archivist at Doncaster.

• East Riding Archive and Local Studies Service, County Hall, Beverley HU17 9BA; tel: 01482 392790; email: archives.service@eastriding .gov.uk; website: www.eastriding.gov.uk.
Some references to flax mills, such as Taylor, Broomer & Co. (solicitors' records include sketch plan of Staddlethorpe Flax Mills of the Oliver family, flax merchant). Yorkshire Flax Ltd – an original bundle relating to the Hull Flax and Cotton Mill Co. c. 1840–1859 (liquidation). There is a lease of a flax-spinning mill in Wilsell, 1828. Claims for bounty on flax grown in the years 1788 and 1789 with a list of claimants with original documents. Hall's Barton Ropery Ltd, Overton Bros Wire Ropes Ltd, Beverley, has general papers but no personal details. Deeds and documents that sometimes refer to textile workers, for example, the admission of Robert Demaine of Pateley Bridge, linen weaver and bleacher, and Michael Gamlin of Otley, cotton manufacturer, as devisees in trust of Thomas Horner of Pateley Bridge, linen weaver 1795; will of Joseph Potts of Sculcoates, sailcloth manufacturer 1822; and in the Lister papers is an assignment for the benefit of creditors of Christopher Lister of Snaith, hosier and worsted manufacturer 1831.

• Hull City Archives, 79 Lowgate, Hull HU1 1HN; tel: 01482 615102; email: City.Archives@hullcc.gov.uk; website: www.hullcc.gov.uk/ portal/page?_pageid=221,52893and_dad=portaland_schema=PORTAL. Mostly deeds and individual documents, such as an assignment of 1895 W N Jameson of Hull, hemp and flax manufacturer, apprenticeship indentures, such as that of John Sherwood, son of Mary Sherwood of Hull to John Pearson of Hull, rope maker 1808, and a lease (indent) 1834 William Locking of Hull, lace manufacturer.

• North Yorkshire County Record Office, Malpas Road, Northallerton DL7 8TB; tel: 01609 777585; email: archives@northyorks.gov.uk; website: www.northyorks.gov.uk/archives.
Examples include Peter Green & Company, wool textile weavers (twentieth-century correspondence and papers relating to orders for cloth), letters and circulars from the Household Textile Association,

Manchester, to Messrs Walton and Company Limited, Castle Mills, Knaresborough 1950–1954, handbills relating to linen manufacture in Ripon 1785–1835 and hemp and flax bounty claims papers 1781–1797.

• Sheffield Archives, 52 Shoreham Street, Sheffield S1 4SP; tel: 01142 03 9395; email: archives@sheffield.gov.uk; website: www.sheffield.gov.uk/archives.

A variety of documents, including the accounts of Matthew Ashton, a Hamburg cloth merchant 1681–1693, deeds involving Jersey weavers, Henry and John Webster 1748, papers of the Gardom family (Gardom and Pares, cotton spinners, of Calver Mill). The surrender of a lease 1825, John Laycock, of Sheffield, hair-seating manufacturer, to the burgesses. A mortgage 1801, John Pickering, the younger, late of Barnsley, Yorkshire, but now of Red Brooke, parish of Darton, linen manufacturer together with his will dated 1810.

• West Yorkshire Archive Service, Wakefield Headquarters, Registry of Deeds, Newstead Road, Wakefield WF1 2DE; tel: 01924 305980; website: www.archives.wyjs.org.uk.

Extensive records. Examples include an order to the Constable of Attercliffe to ensure appearance of three illegal linen weavers at the next sessions 20 July 1675: John Oakes, Dinis Broadbent and John Sowerby of Attercliffe who had practised the trade without having served the required seven-year apprenticeship and a traverse of the case against John Oakes and John Sowerby of Attercliffe January 1676. Returns by masters of cotton mills with more than three apprentices, some concerning more than one mill; two reports of mill visitors, includes the report of Thomas Bayliffe, Vicar of Rotherham and visitor of mills in the wapentake of Upper Strafforth and Tickhill, on 'the Sheffield cotton mill'. Quarter Sessions Summary Convictions 1778–1811 and 1856–1916 refer to those accused of fraud against the wool masters. July 1781–October 1785 copy returns of claimants of flax and hemp bounties: this is indexed under 'hemp and flax'. Those for January 1789–October 1791 include a statement of claims for flax bounty – Michaelmas sessions, 1790. Records of unions such as those of the National Union of Dyers, Bleachers and Textile Workers and of manufacturers such as the Committee of Worsted Manufacturers for the counties of York, Lancaster and Chester, minutes 1777–1804 (microfilm copy). Records of solicitors such as those of Eaton Smith & Downey contain many references to textile manufacturers.

• West Yorkshire Archive Service, Bradford, Bradford Central Library, Prince's Way, Bradford BD1 1NN; email: bradford@wyjs.org.uk; website: www.archives.wyjs.org.uk.

Many records of Bradford businesses, such as Edelstein, Moser & Co., worsted coating and woollen manufacturers, and Sir James Hill and Sons Ltd, Keighley, topmakers (records of salaries 1924–1969 and includes details of Sir James Hill's golden-wedding bonus with complete list of employees with years of service 1924). Union records, such as the Bradford Dyers Association, records 1898–1962 and Amalgamated Union of Dyers, Finishers, Bleachers and Kindred Trades, as well as manufacturers' organisations such as the Worsted Committee of Yorkshire, Lancashire and Chester, including minutes 1777–1950, subscription lists 1897–1937, accounts 1777–1942 and records of cases or offences for Keighley, Bradford, Leeds, Colne and Halifax districts 1823–1876 and the Wool Textile Manufacturing Federation Ltd, of Bradford, includes minutes for a range of manufacturers' associations in the West Riding. There is a transcript of sixteenth-century–seventeenth-century Bradford Court Rolls compiled for J Norton Dickons, Bradford, antiquarian in 1912.

• West Yorkshire Archive Service, Calderdale, Central Library, Northgate House, Northgate, Halifax HX1 1UN; tel: 01422 392636; email: calderdale@wyjs.org.uk; website: www.archives.wyjs.org.uk.

Records include areas that may now be in neighbouring administrative areas since the reorganisation of 1974.

Example records include an indenture for Thomas Green, Barnoldswick, and Robert Green, his father, yeoman to Alan Edmundson, Barnoldswick, linen weaver 12 May 1698. There are extensive records for Fielden Brothers Ltd, Todmorden 1626–1990, including articles and records of share formation 1889–1972; minutes of meetings 1889–1967; registers of members 1900–1966; share records 1890–1987; title deeds for Langfield, Stansfield, Todmorden-cum-Walsden and elsewhere 1626–1990; personnel records 1842–1985, including wage and salary records 1842–1985; plans 1842–c. 1965; Todmorden Valley Mill owners' records 1803–1948. Equally extensive are the records for John Crossley & Sons Ltd, Halifax. Records for Cords Ltd, Corduroy and Fustian Manufacturers, Pecket Well Mill, Wadsworth, include weavers' cloth day books 1936–1970 and wages books 1955–1968. This was the last fustian-weaving mill in Hebden Bridge when it closed in 1998.

• West Yorkshire Archive Service, Kirklees, Central Library, Princess Alexandra Walk, Huddersfield HD1 2SU; tel: 01484 221966; email: kirklees@wyjs.org.uk; website: www.archives.wyjs.org.uk.

There is a large collection relating to all aspects of the textile industry, all listed on the A2A website, including a petition in support of plans to build a fulling mill in 1709 signed by forty-two people. The collection for Field & Bottrill, Skelmanthorpe, includes register and certificate of fitness of employees 1886–1902, while those of G & J Stubley Ltd, Batley, include registers of children employed 1867–1912. The Red House Museum collection, Gomersal, has apprentices' indentures for the textile industry 1847 and 1868. Kirklees Archives also has a large collection of apprentice indentures for surrounding townships.

Many landowners' papers include deeds, etc. involving textile workers but some of these are still held by the individual land owner. Kirklees Archives can advise on this or details may be found on the A2A website.

• Keighley Public Library, North Street, Keighley BD21 3SX; tel: 01535 618215.

Township records, which include apprenticeship papers 1664–1832, settlement and removal papers and list of wool combers employed by Abraham Wildman, worsted manufacturer 1835 and 1837. Keighley Business Records is a miscellaneous collection including the time register and register of workers under Factories Acts of Frederick Merrall, weavers, of Steeton Mills and certificates issued under the Factory Act for children employed 1840–1865, Factory Act register 1837–1844, wage books 1836–1846 for John Brigg and Co. of Keighley.

• West Yorkshire Archive Service, Leeds, Chapeltown Road, Sheepscar, Leeds LS7 3AP; tel: 01132 145814; email: leeds@wyjs.org.uk; website: www.archives.wyjs.org.uk.

Some Court Rolls of Knaresborough that include references to linen weavers, as well as deeds, bonds, mortgages, wills, etc. that include textile workers.

• York City Archives Department, Art Gallery Building, Exhibition Square, York YO1 7EW; tel: 01904 551878/9; email: archives@ york.gov.uk; website: www.york.gov.uk/libraries/archives/index.html.

Records include an index of craft workers and a register of York Freemen 1680–1986 by John Malden (this contains an index of occupations). There are two volumes relating to the York Company of Silkweavers and later records of the York & District Guild of Spinners, Weavers and Dyers 1950–1990s and 2005–2006.

• Yorkshire Archaeological Society, Claremont, 23 Clarendon Road, Leeds LS2 9NZ; tel: 01132 456362; email: yas@wyjs.org.uk; website: www.archives.wyjs.org.uk.
Holds many deeds and documents that may have references to occupations, such as the 1883 will of Andrew Pickard, woollen manufacturer, Leeds and Ossett, and articles of agreement relating to Felling Closes and cotton manufactory 1790 by Robert Taylor of Giggleswick, cotton manufacturer.

• University of Bradford, Special Collections Library, J B Priestley Library, University of Bradford, Bradford BD7 1DP; tel: 01274 235256; email: a.cullingford@bradford.ac.uk; website: www.bradford.ac.uk/library/special.
This has various rare books and archives relating to the history of dyeing and wool textile industries in Bradford, including papers of the Holden family.

The Archive of the Bradford Technical College has records relating to individuals ONLY if they attended the College or are otherwise well known in the textile industry.

Bradford Textile Archive is due to be relocated from Bradford College to Salts Mill at Saltaire to form part of a new Textile Archive housed there. The archive relates primarily to the storage and display of fabrics. For up-to-date details of the Bradford Textile Archive access the website: www.cbwt.co.uk/new/archivenewsletter1.pdf.

• Borthwick Institute for Archives, University of York, Heslington, York YO10 5DD; email: bihr500@york.ac.uk; website: www.york.ac.uk/borthwick.
Wide range of records. For example, records of the Company of the Staple, which include a Royal Charter 1669; minute books 1619–1927; meetings, agenda and reports 1828–1961; papers regarding Company officers 1772–1799; membership lists 1913, 1923 and 1949–1950. The Borthwick Institute for Archives at the University of York holds photocopies of many medieval deeds, account rolls, rentals and of minutes for the period 1677–1985. Deeds and documents usually mention occupations, e.g., an exchange of lands and tithe rent charges

(copy) 1873 between William Williams, Vicar of Whitgift, clerk and Thomas Ounsley of Reedness, flax merchant.

• Special Collections, Leeds University Library, Woodhouse Lane, Leeds, West Yorkshire LS2 9JT; tel: 01133 435518 or 01133 436383; email: special-collections@library.leeds.ac.uk; website: www.leeds.ac.uk/library/spcoll/index.htm.
In Special Collections there is a wide range of material connected to the textile and other industries, but not all company records contain staff details.

At www.leeds.ac.uk/library/spcoll/index.htm scroll down to 'All materials in Special Collections (main library catalogue)' and type in the keyword 'business'. This will bring up a list of all business records held in the library. There is also a list of PDF handlists, which describe specific collections, which can be found at the bottom of the homepage on the website.

• Library and Computing Services, University of Huddersfield Queensgate, Huddersfield HD1 3DH; tel: 01484 473888; email: lc@hud.ac.uk.
This holds the archive of the Huddersfield Mechanics' Institute (1843–1884), Huddersfield Technical School and Mechanics' Institution (1884–1896) and Huddersfield Female Educational Institute (1846–1883), all with some records of students and members.

A number of transcripts from early records are available, such as F W Dendy's extracts from the records of the Merchant Adventurers of Newcastle upon Tyne, Vol ii and copies of work by Maud Sellers on the York Mercers and Merchant Adventurers 1356–1917. Selections from the records of the companies, mainly from the sixteenth century, the earlier items in Latin, with a glossary. The latest extract is dated 1827; list of governors ends 1917. Extracts from the Hull custom rolls and complete transcripts of ulnagers' rolls can be found in John Lister (ed.), *The Early Yorkshire Woollen Trade. Extracts from the Hull customs' rolls, transcripts of the ulnager's rolls* (Yorkshire Archaeological Society, Record Series, 64, 1924).

There is a large local history section of books and magazines, including *Yorkshire Factory Times*, *The Dyer and Colourist* 1899–1977 and *Textile Manufacturer* 1887–1950, as well as early newspapers available on microfiche or film.

The G H Wood Collection covers much of the history of the local textile industry. Wood was the Secretary of the Huddersfield and District Woollen Manufacturers and Spinners Association from 1907.

• Armley Mills Industrial Museum, Armley Mills, Canal Road, Armley, Leeds LS12 2QF; tel: 01132 637861; email: armley.mills@leeds.gov.uk.
Housed in a former textile mill, machinery and other exhibits demonstrate working life. Also, has some records, including Hepworth Tailoring, Leeds-based clothing manufacturers. Archive is principally photographs.

• Bankfield Museum, Boothtown Road, Halifax HX3 6HG; tel: 01422 35 4823/35; website: www.calderdale.gov.uk/leisure/museums-galleries/bankfield-museum.
Also has records relating to Clay and Horsfall, worsted spinners, J T Clay and Sons Ltd, Hind Robinson and Son Ltd, John Murgatroyd and Son Ltd, T Pickles and Sons, Leyland Roberts, botanist, fl. 1822–1847. These are principally pattern and financial books. Also, costume and textile exhibition.

• Bradford Industrial Museum and Horses at Work, Moorside Mills, Moorside Road, Eccleshill, Bradford BD2 3HP; tel: 01274 435900; email: industrial.museum@bradford.gov.uk.
Some archives, mostly samples, pattern books, plans and business books rather than specific details of personnel. Records of Bulmer and Lumb, worsted spinners and manufacturers of Prospect Mills, Wibsey; George Lee and Sons Ltd, private ledgers.
An excellent display of machinery and often has working demonstrations, as well as exhibits relating to the textile industry.

• Merchant Adventurers' Company, Merchant Adventurers' Hall, Fossgate, York YO1 9XD; tel: 01904 652243; email: archivist@ theyorkcompany.co.uk; website: www.theyorkcompany .co.uk.
In addition to the historic buildings there are some archives, such as records of admissions of members and apprentices and contains documents dating from the early 1200s up to the present day. It has hundreds of original medieval charters, including, among other documents, records of admissions of members and apprentices, trade papers and minute books and records of the York residences of the Merchant Adventurers of England and of the Eastland Merchants. Access to the original documents for academic research is by

appointment only and enquiries should be made to the Assistant Archivist at the Hall.

Chapter 13

PLACES TO VISIT AND WEBSITES BY AREA

The textile industry is now part of our 'heritage' and as such has spawned museums and history trails. All these can be very useful as background information about the conditions in which ancestors worked, but you may also be lucky and find some reference to a specific individual as well as the business itself.

13.1 East Midlands

• Boot and Shoe Collection, Central Museum and Art Gallery, Guildhall Road, Northampton NN1 1DP; tel: 01604 838111; website: www.northampton.gov.uk/museums.
The history of footwear: shoe making, retailing, specialist shoes and foot health.

• Carpet Museum Trust, The Weaver's Loft, New Meeting Church, Church Street, Kidderminster DY10 1AQ; website: www.carpet museum.co.uk.
Small exhibition of artefacts. Also has an archive of documents from the carpet industry in the area. To use the archive contact Carpet Archives Centre Unit 28 – MCF Complex, 60 New Road, Kidderminster DY10 1AQ; website: www.carpetmuseum.co.uk. There is an online catalogue.

• Cromford Mill, Mill Lane, Cromford, Derbyshire DE4 3RQ; website: www.arkwrigthsociety.co.uk.
No records as such held, but provides good background to the textile industry.

• Derby's Museum of Industry and History, Silk Mill Lane, off Full Street, Derby E1 3AF; tel: 01332 255308; website: www.derby.gov.uk /museums/.

• Derwent Valley Visitor Centre, North Mill, Bridgefoot, Belper, Derbyshire DE56 1YD; tel/fax: 01773 880474; email: info@ belper northmill.org.uk; website: www.belpernorthmill.org/.

• Masson Mills, Derby Road , Matlock Bath, Derbyshire DE4 3PY; tel: 01629 581001 (enquiries and bookings); website: www.massonmills. co.uk/.

• Museum of Costume and Textiles, 51 Castle Gate, Nottingham NG1 6AF; tel: 01159 153500/3541.

• The Museum of Nottingham Life at Brewhouse Yard Museum, Castle Boulevard, Nottingham NG7 1FB; tel: 01159 153600.

• Nottingham Industrial Museum, Wollaton Park, Courtyard Stables, Wollaton, Nottingham NG8 2AE; tel: 01159 153900; email: wollaton @ncmg.demon.co.uk.

• Ruddington Framework Knitters Museum, Chapel Street, Ruddington, Nottingham NG11 6HE; website: www.rfkm.org.uk/.

• Wigston Framework Knitters Museum, 42/44 Bushloe End, Wigston, Leicester LE18 2BA.

Useful websites

• www.derwentvalleymills.org/index.htm – explains the history and development of textiles in this area.

• www.knittingtogether.org.uk/ – an excellent website for anyone with an interest in East Midlands textiles.

• www.northants-familytree.net/indexes.html – militia lists of Northamptonshire.

13.2 Eastern England

• Braintree District Museum, Manor Street, Braintree CM7 3HW; tel: 01376 325266.
'Threads of Time' tells the story of Braintree's textile heritage from the medieval wool trade to modern times.

• Bridewell Museum of Norwich, Bridewell Alley, Norwich NR2 1AQ; tel: 01603 667228; website: www.museums.norfolk.gov.uk/ default. asp?Document=200.22.

• Carrow House Costume and Textile Study Centre, Carrow House, 301 King Street, Norwich NR1 2TS; tel: 01603 228870; website: www.norfolk.gov.uk/tourism/museums/carrow.
Includes beadwork.

• Coggeshall Museum and Heritage Centre, Village Hall, Stoneham Street, Coggeshall, Essex CO6 1UH; tel: 01376 563003; email: spratcliffe@btinternet.com; website: www.geocities.com/coggeshall museum.

Paradise Mill, Macclesfield.

• Fitzwilliam Museum, Trumpington Street, Cambridge CB2 1RB; tel: 01223 332900; website: www.fitzmuseum.cam.ac.uk.
Includes rugs and samplers.

• Curator of Costume and Textiles, Manor House Museum, Honey Hill, Bury St Edmunds, Suffolk I33 1HF; tel: 01284 757076; website: www.stedmundsbury.gov.uk.
Fine embroideries and costume.

• Wardown Park Museum (formerly Luton Museum and Gallery), Wardown Park, Luton, Bedfordshire LU2 7HA; tel: 01582 546722; website: www.luton.gov.uk/museums.
Focuses on the women's hat industry.

• Warner Textile Archive, Warners Mill, Silks Way, Braintree, Essex CM7 3GB; tel: 01376 557741; email: warner.archive@braintree.gov.uk.
Correspondence: Ann Wise, Warner Archive Development and Licensing Manager, c/o Town Hall Centre, Market Place, Braintree, CM7 3YG; email: ann.wise@braintree.gov.uk.

Useful websites

• www.greatbardfield-pc.gov.uk/the_museum.htm – exhibitions of straw plaiting.

13.3 North East

• Otterburn Mills Ltd, Otterburn, Northumberland NE19 1JT; tel: 01830 520225; website: www.otterburnmill.co.uk/.
The Otterburn Tweed Mill was established in 1821, only ceasing full production at the end of the twentieth century, and it still operates on a small scale as part of the tourist industry. Now a clothing outlet, it also has an exhibition of textile machinery and other items relating to the textile trade.

13.4 North West

• Dent Heritage Centre, Dent, Cumbria LA10 5QJ; tel: 01539 625800; website: www.dentvillageheritagecentre.co.uk.
Shows the story of Dentdale from its past to the present day, with one section given to the knitting industry of the area.

• Farfield Mill, Garsdale Road, Sedbergh, Cumbria LA10 5LW; tel: 01539 621958; email: themanager@farfieldmill.org; website: www.farfieldmill .org.
Arts and heritage centre in former woollen-mill complex.

• Fells and Dales, The Old Stables, Redhills, Penrith CA11 0DT; tel: 01768 869533; email: info@fellsanddales.org.uk; website: www.fellsanddales .org.uk.

• Hat Works Museum, Wellington Mill, Wellington Road South, Stockport, Cheshire SK3 0EU; tel: 01613 557773; website: www. hatworks.org.uk.
As well as the museum collection there is a small hat-book library and a collection of related documents and hatting ephemera, which may be viewed by appointment. These relate mainly to the local men's fur felt-hatting industry.

• Helmshore Mills Textile Museum, Holcombe Road, Helmshore, Rossendale BB4 4NP; tel: 01706 226459; email: helmshore.museum @mus.lancscc.gov.uk; website: www.lancashire.gov.uk/education /museums/helmshore/index.asp.

• Lakeland Sheep and Wool Centre, Cockermouth, Cumbria CA13 0QX; tel/fax: 01900 822673; email: reception@sheep-woolcentre.co.uk; website: www.sheep-woolcentre.co.uk.
Heritage centre with sheepdog displays at certain times.

• Macclesfield Silk Museum, The Silk Industry Museum, Park Lane, Macclesfield SK11 6TJ; tel: 01625 612045; website: www.macclesfield .silk.museum.
The library has some business-related items, including some biographical details, an oral-history collection, over 30,000 images of varying sorts, a range of newspapers from the eighteenth to mid-twentieth century and a large number of detailed maps of the local area. An appointment must be made to visit the library.

• Museum of Lakeland Life, Abbot Hall, Kendal, Cumbria LA9 5AL; tel: 01539 722464; email: info@lakelandmuseum.org.uk; website: www.lakelandmuseum.org.uk.

Information and displays on sheep farming and woollen textile manufacture.

• Queen Street Mill, Harle Syke, Burnley BB10 2HX; tel: 01282 412555; email: queenstreet.mill@mus.lancscc.gov.uk; website: www.lancashire. gov.uk/education/museums/queen/index.asp.
Library and small amount of archives available by appointment only.

• Stott Park Bobbin Mill, Finsthwaite, Ulverston, Cumbria LA12 8AX; tel: 01539 531087.

• The Weavers' Triangle Visitor Centre, 85 Manchester Road, Burnley B11 1JZ; tel: 01282 452403; website: www.weaverstriangle.co.uk.

• Working Class Movement Library, 51 The Crescent , Salford M5 4WX; tel: 01617 363601; website: www.wcml.org.uk/.

Useful websites

• www.cottontown.org/page.cfm?pageid=257 – history of cotton in the north west.

• www.spinningtheweb.org.uk/ – excellent website that also has a bibliography giving details of sources throughout the north west. Principally relates to cotton/north west of England.

13.5 South East

• Bedford Museum, Castle Lane, Bedford MK40 3XD; tel: 01243 53323; email: bmuseum@bedford.gov.uk; website: www.bedfordmuseum.org. Bedford and its surrounding villages are famous for their traditional Bedfordshire lace made with bobbins. The Museum houses a small collection of lace, as well as lace-making equipment, in particular lace prickings and a large collection of the traditional East Midlands bobbins.

• Bexley Museums, Hall Place and Gardens, Bourne Road, Bexley DA5 1PQ.
The extensive archive of David Evans & Co., Silk Printers, Dyers and Finishers of Crayford became part of the collection in 2001 with the closure of the Company's factory. The collection contains a variety of

items from the nineteenth- and twentieth-century textile-printing industry, including plastic mixing jugs, wooden casting blocks, silk screens, fabric samples, pattern books and other items from the Company's premises.

• Carisbrooke Castle Museum, Newport P030 1XY; tel: 01983 523112; email: carismus@lineone.net; website: www.carisbrookecastlemuseum .org.uk/default.aspx.
Examples of embroidered net, probably made at the Newport lace factory, and Isle of Wight lace pattern book.

• The Cowper and Newton Museum, Orchard Side, Market Place, Olney, Buckinghamshire MK46 4AJ; tel: 01234 711516; email: cnm@mkheritage.co.uk; website: www.mkheritage.co.uk/cnm/index .html.

• Gosport Discovery Centre, High Street, Gosport, Hampshire PO12 1BT; tel: 08456 035631.

• Maidstone Museum and Bentlif Art Gallery, St Faiths Street, Maidstone ME14 1LH; tel: 01622 754497; website: www.museum. maidstone.gov.uk.

• Mill Green Museum and Mill, Mill Green, Hatfield AL9 5PD; tel: 01701 271362; email: museum@welhat.gov.uk; website: www.herts museums.org.uk/millgreen.

• The Wandle Industrial Museum, The Vestry Hall Annexe, London Road, Mitcham, Surrey CR4 3UD; tel: 02086 480127; website: www. wandle.org.uk/common/frame.htm.

• Wardown Park Museum (formerly Luton Museum and Gallery), Wardown Park, Luton, Bedfordshire LU2 7HA; tel: 01582 546722; website: www.luton.gov.uk/museums.
Focus on the women's hat industry with over 600 hats on display.

• Whitchurch Silk Mill, 28 Winchester Street, Whitchurch, Hampshire RG28 7AL; tel: 01256 892065; email: silkmill@btinternet.com; website: www.whitchurchsilkmill.org.uk.

Useful websites

• www.witneyblanketstory.org.uk – excellent website telling the full story of blanket making and many of the firms involved in it.

• www.wandle.org.uk/common/framez.htm – gives extensive history of mills in the Wandle Valley area.

• www.eastlondonhistory.com/huguenots.htm – information about Huguenots who settled in London.

• www.witney.net/history.htm – information about Witney and its textile industry.

• www.cotton-threads.org.uk/ – the story of the Hutchinson family of Broom Hall.

13.6 London

• Jewish Museum, The Sternberg Centre, 80 East End Road, Finchley, London N3 2SY; tel: 02083 491143.
Information about Jewish history and the arrival of Jews in Britain, which helps give pointers for tracing Jewish ancestry.

• The Museum of Immigration and Diversity, 19 Princelet Street, London E1 6QH; tel: 0207 247 5352; email: information@ 19princeletstreet.org.uk.
Housed in what was once a Huguenot silk-weaver's house and then a Jewish synagogue.

• Victoria & Albert Museum, Cromwell Road, London SW7 2RL; tel: 0207 942 2000; website: www.vam.ac.uk/.
Holds a unique collection of textiles from all over the world, from all eras. The National Art Library at the museum (www.vam.ac.uk/nal) has a large collection of books relating to textiles.

• Museum of London, 150 London Wall, London EC2Y 5HN; tel: 08704 443852; website: www.museumoflondon.org.uk.
Includes social and working history sections with examples of silk weaving, braid making and a collection of medieval cloth seals, which were attached to bales of cloth when they were imported.

13.7 South West

• Coldharbour Mill, Uffculme, Cullompton EX15 3EE; tel: 01884 840960; website: www.coldharbourmill.org.uk.
Holds the Coldharbour Mill staff records 1879–1940. The firm produced khaki cloth for the Army and employed many people in the area.

• Cotswolds Woollen Weavers, Filkins, Nr Lechlade, Gloucestershire GL7 3JJ; tel: 01367 860491; website: www.thecotswoldgateway.co.uk/cotswolds-woollen-weavers.htm.
A working mill and museum that produces garments and cloth for sale in the mill shop with displays detailing the story of Cotswold wool.

• Tiverton Museum, St Andrew Street, Tiverton EX16 6PH; correspondence address: Tiverton and Mid Devon Museum Trust, Becks Square, Tiverton EX16 6PJ; tel: 01884 256295; email: research@tivertonmuseum.org.uk; website: www.tivertonmuseum.org.uk.

• Trowbridge Museum, The Shires, Court Street, Trowbridge, Wiltshire; tel: 01225 751339; email: info@trowbridgemuseum.co.uk; website: www.trowbridgemuseum.co.uk/.

13.8 Wales

• Greenfield Valley Heritage Park, Basingwerk House, Greenfield Valley, Greenfield, Holywell, Flintshire CH8 7GH; tel: 01352 714172; email: info@greenfieldvalley.com; website: www.greenfieldvalley.com.

• Llanidloes Museum, The Town Hall, Great Oak Street, Llanidloes SY18 6BN; tel: 01686 413777; website: powysmuseums.powys.gov.uk.

• Melin Tregwynt Mill, Castlemorris, Pembrokeshire SA62 5UX; tel: 08700 424199; website: www.melintregwynt.co.uk/.

• Museum of Welsh Life, St Fagans, Cardiff CF5 6XB; tel: 02920 573500; website: www.museumwales.ac.uk/en/cardiff.
Records of Jacob Jones & Son, tweed and cloth manufacturers,

1886–1939: account books (four), diaries (nine), certificates and miscellaneous papers.

• National Wool Museum, Dre-fach Felindre, Near Newcastle Emlyn, Llandysul, Carmarthenshire SA44 5UP; tel: 01559 370929; website: www.museumwales.ac.uk/en/wool.

• Newtown Textile Museum, 5–7 Commercial Street, Newtown, Powys SY16 2BL; tel: 01686 622024; website: www.powys.gov.uk.

• Solva Woollen Mill, Middle Mill, Solva, Haverfordwest, Pembrokeshire SA62 6XD; tel: 01437 721112; email: enquiries@ solvawoollenmill.co.uk; website: www.solvawoollenmill.co.uk/index2 .htm.

Dre-fach Felindre Museum, Carmarthenshire.

Useful websites

• www.archivesnetworkwales.info – covers all Welsh repositories.

• history.powys.org.uk/school1/primhome.shtml – website giving brief history of various towns in Powys (Montgomeryshire, Radnorshire and Breconshire), including references to various woollen and flannel mills.

• www.welsh-costume.co.uk/woollenindustrylinks.php – gives links to many sites concerned with the Welsh woollen industry.

13.9 Yorkshire

• Calderdale Industrial Museum, Central Works, Square Rd, Halifax HX1 0QG; tel: 01422 358087.
Collections covering a hundred years of local industry, including some working machines.

• Colne Valley Museum, Cliffe Ash, Golcar, Huddersfield HD7 4PY; tel: 01484 659762; website: www.colnevalleymuseum.org.uk/.
Three nineteenth-century weavers' cottages combined to house the Colne Valley Museum. The restored rooms show the life and work of the nineteenth century.

• Colour Museum, Perkin House, PO Box 244, Providence Street, Bradford BD1 2PW; tel: 01274 390955.
Visits to the Bradford site are by appointment only.

• W R Outhwaite & Son Ropemakers, Town Foot, Hawes, North Yorkshire DL8 3NT; tel: 01969 667487; email: info@ropemakers.co.uk.
Visitor centre showing how ropes are made.

• Salts Mill, Shipley, Saltaire, West Yorkshire BD18 3LA; tel: 01274 531163; email: post@saltsmill.org.uk.
Titus Salt's mill, now a shopping complex and art gallery. It is located in the village of Saltaire, which Salt built for his workers.

Useful websites

• www.calderdale.gov.uk/wtw/index.html – from 'Weaver to Web', an online visual archive of Calderdale.

Colne Valley Museum, Huddersfield.

• www.colour-experience.org/ – this website is run by the Society of Dyers and Colourists, and gives information about dyeing and the textile industry.

• www.cottontown.org – includes the history of cotton and some wool/worsted in Yorkshire.

GLOSSARY

alnager, aulnager, ulnagar
Official who measured/examined cloth for quality and affixed an official seal.

annatto maker
Made dyes.

bass or bast dresser
Dressed fibre or matting.

beam
A large spool, about 1m in diameter, on which warp is wound.

beamer
Someone who winds warp onto the beam before putting it onto the loom.

beater
A fuller or walker who washed and thickened cloth by treading it in water with fuller's earth.

beaver
Made the felt used in hat making.

blending
Mixing grades or shades of wool together to get overall grade of wool.

bobbin
A spool that can be placed on a spindle. It is used to hold yarn for spinning or weaving.

bombazine
Twilled silk and worsted fabric, often used for mourning clothes.

bowker
Bleacher of yarn.

broad-cloth weaver
Operated a wide loom.

buckram
Stiff finished cotton or linen used for linings of garments.

burling
Picking over cloth to remove bits, etc.

calico
A fabric made from unbleached, and often not fully processed, cotton.

carding
The cleaning and mixing of fibres to produce a continuous sliver suitable for processing. The fibres are passed on rollers between moving wires or teeth.

carding engineer
Operated and maintained the carding machines that cleaned and mixed fibres

to produce a continuous sliver suitable for processing.

chapman
Copeman, ceapman – a seventeenth- or eighteenth-century merchant who took raw wool or cotton to outworkers for them to spin and weave on piece rates. The chapman then sold the cloth for a profit; also a peddler.

cheese
A roll of yarn on a paper or wooden tube that resembles a large cheese.

cloth looker
'Quality control' inspector who looked at the finished cloth to see if there were any faults – could remedy slight faults or pass to menders.

combing
For worsted cloth – fibres were combed smooth.

cone
Tapered cylinder around which yarn is wound.

cotton gasser
Worked in the 'gas room' where cotton was gassed or fumigated to purify it, or one who applied gas to cotton yarn to make it smoother.

creel
The rack for holding packs of yarn on a textile machine.

cropping
Raising the nap on cloth, then cutting it short to improve the finish. Originally done with heavy shears, then machinery.

cut
Length of fabric or warp. One cut was about 80yd (72m). Later warps might be prepared in multiples of 80yd.

danter
Female overseer in winding room of a silk mill.

deviller
Operated a 'devil' machine, which tore rags into small pieces.

doubling
Twisting of threads together to form a stronger and thicker yarn.

drawboy
Assisted a weaver in the shawl industry – sat on top of the loom and lifted the heavy warps.

dresser
Prepared yarns ready for weaving – silk dresser, flax dresser, etc.

drysalter
Dealer in dyes for the textile industry.

engine tenter
Operated/maintained the steam engine and boiler in a mill.

felt
Fabric is a compact sheet of entangled, not woven, wool, fur and sometimes cotton fibres. The felt is produced by treating a mat of fibres with moisture, heat and pressure.

fent dealer
Seller of 'fents', which were ends of cloth sold cheaply.

fettler
One who removed the rest of the dirt and fluff from the carding machines.

fine woollen trade
Uses short-staple fibres and produces high-quality cloth.

finish mender
More experienced mender responsible for final checking.

flax dresser
Prepared the flax for spinning.

flock
Very short fibres, mainly used to produce textured wallpaper.

framework knitter
Operated a machine that made knitted hosiery. Often seen as an abbreviation – FWK.

fulling/milling
This applies to woollens not worsteds and involves the pounding of cloth in large troughs of warm water and soap to produce a felted cloth.

gigger
Operated gig machines, which brushed and raised the nap of cloth using teasels.

hackler
Hackman, heckler, hetcher, hatcheller. Worked in the linen trade separating the coarse part of flax using a heckle or hackle.

hairweaver
Weaver of cloth made from horsehair.

half-timer
Child who worked half a day in the mill and then went to school for the other half of the day.

heald maker
Heald/yell/yeddle manufacturer – made the healds for the looms.

healding
Passing threads through healds (vertical wires with eyelets).

heck maker
Maker of the part of the spinning machine that guides the yarn onto the reels.

hose manufacturer
Made stockings.

kemp
Coarse animal hair mixed with wool, which shows up in a finished yarn or fabric as a lighter colour or to give texture. A yarn or cloth containing kemp is called kempy.

lace drawer
Drew out the threads during the lace-making process, often a child.

lease bands
A metal or wooden rod that was inserted in the lease to prevent the warp yarn from becoming tangled and to help the right thread to be selected when the warp is being put onto the loom.

lindsey or linsey/woolsey
Coarse linen and wool blend.

liner
Lyner – flax dresser.

loom
Machine that produces woven fabrics.

low woollen trade
Re-uses waste material.

Manchester warehouseman
Warehouseman in a cotton factory.

mender
Highly skilled worker who corrected faults in cloth. Small breaks in the yarn or mis-weaves could be corrected invisibly. Always a woman's job.

mill engineer
Maintained the boiler and engines that powered the whole mill, as well as the mill machinery.

milling/fulling
This applies to woollens not worsteds and involves the pounding of cloth in large troughs of warm water and soap to produce a felted cloth.

mule
A multi-spindle spinning machine developed by Samuel Crompton in 1779.

narrow weaver
Made ribbons, tapes, etc.

orrice weaver
Wove lace patterns in silk thread or in silk cloth.

owler
Wool smuggler.

pack-thread spinner
Operated a machine that made strong thread or twine.

pattern weaver
Wove small, square samples of patterns to show potential buyers. Usually done on small handlooms (worsted) or powerlooms (woollens).

perch
A wooden frame over which a fabric was draped and inspected for faults, illuminated from behind by natural or artificial light. 'To perch' is the action of inspecting the cloth, done by a percher.

pick
Single-weft thread in a fabric.

piece
An accepted unit length of fabric, ranging from 30m to 100m.

piecer
Usually a child who had to twist together broken threads on the loom.

power-loom tuner
Powerloom overlooker – superintended looms, repairing and quality checking them, etc.

raddle
A wooden bar with a row of upright pegs set in it, used by warpers to keep the warp at a proper width, and prevent tangling when it was wound upon the warping balloon.

raff merchant
Sold raffia.

rag picker
Sorted rags into types for re-use.

reacher
Reacher-in – worker who fed the individual threads through the healds.

reed
The reed is a bar that spreads the warp threads across the width of the fabric. After the weft has passed through the warp threads, the reed is pulled back to beat it into position.

sailcloth
A strong, heavy canvas or duck made in plain weave.

sarcinet weaver
Silk weaver.

scouring
Washing the cloth or yarn with fuller's earth, or more modern chemicals, to remove oil, natural grease, dirt, etc.

scribbler
Operated the combing machine used in one of the early wool/cotton processes.

sharman
Shearman, sherman, cropper – raised the nap then sheared it smooth to finish the cloth.

shed
An opening formed during weaving by raising some warp threads and lowering others. The shuttle is then sent through the shed with the weft.

shoddy
Poor-quality, re-used wool.

shuttle
Part of a loom that carries yarn back and forth across the fabric width. It contains a spool of yarn called a bobbin.

silk drawer
Produced silk from silk waste, ready to make into thread.

silk thrower
Silk throwster – made the thread ready for spinning.

sizer
Applies size to thread to strengthen it, usually to use as warp.

sleying
Connecting warp threads through reeds in the centre of the loom (keeps threads in place and drives home the weft after each pick).

slubber doffer
Doffer – removed the bobbins from the spinning machine.

slubbing
Part of carding – fibres are drawn out further and joined together, with a slight twist.

spindle
A metal rod or wooden stick for holding spools, cheeses or bobbins on spinning frames, warping machines, etc.

spinner
Spun and twisted the cleaned and drawn-out raw material into a thread that could be used on a loom. Later this was done on a water-/steam-powered machine.

spinning
Twisting the fibres together to form a strong yarn.

swingler
Operated the machine that separated the coarse parts of flax.

tatting
A form of handmade lace using a small shuttle and thread.

teazing
Loosening the wool fibres before cleaning or spinning.

tentering
Drying and stretching the fabric.

throwster
Twisted strands of yarn together, usually silk.

twist hand
Someone who operated a lace-making machine.

twister
Twisterer – operated the machine that twisted yarn.

twister-in
Right-handed or left-handed – twisted the new yarn to the ends of the yarn already in the machine, which saved time setting up new warps.

warp
Yarns that run along the length of a fabric.

warper
Someone who wound yarn onto warp mill, laying out threads in correct length, width, colours, etc. for the loom.

warping
Winding yarn onto warp mill to lay out threads in correct length, width, colours, etc. for the loom; the yarn was then sized with glue to strengthen,

dried and then put on loom.

weaver
Wove the cloth by interlacing warp and weft threads on a loom.

weft
Yarns that run across the width of a fabric (also known as filling).

willeyer
Someone who operated a willeying machine, which separated the wool fibres, ready for carding.

winder
Transferred the yarn from the bobbins ready for weaving.

wool comber
Someone who operated the combing machine, part of preparing the raw material ready for spinning.

wool factor
Wool merchant's agent.

wool sorter
Wool stapler – sorted wool into different qualities.

woollen cloth
Woven from wool yarns where the fibres have not been combed and lie in all directions. Tends to have a fluffy surface.

worsted cloth
Woven from wool yarns that have been combed to make the fibres parallel. Tends to have a smooth surface.

worsted trade
Uses long-staple fibres.

Useful websites for occupations

• www.rmhh.co.uk/occup/c.html.

• www.genealogyinc.com/enc_occupations/job-F.html.

BIBLIOGRAPHY

The textile industry was so much at the forefront of the Industrial Revolution, and also at its demise, that it has attracted great interest from a range of historians. There are many textbooks available, giving details of each sector of the industry and tracing its rise and fall through the ages. Some concentrate on a specific industry, such as D T Jenkins and K G Ponting, *The British Wool Textile Industry 1770–1914* or A Burton, *The Rise and Fall of King Cotton*. Others provide a broad study of the textile industry, one of the most comprehensive being D Jenkins (ed.), *The Cambridge History of Western Textiles*. See below for a further selection.

Mill architecture has also been investigated and documented. The Royal Commission on the Historical Monuments of England (RCHME), in conjunction with other archaeology services, produced three major studies, resulting in the publication of three titles: C Giles and I H Goodall, *Yorkshire Textile Mills 1770–1930*, M Williams and D A Farnie, *Cotton Mills in Greater Manchester* and A Calladine and J Fricker, *East Cheshire Textile Mills*. See bibliography for a further selection.

Carpets

Bartlett, J N, *Carpeting the Millions: The Growth of Britain's Carpet Industry*, John Donald Publications, n.d.
Shea, W, *Carpet Making in Durham City*, Durham City Council, 1984.
Tattersall, C E C, *History of British Carpets*, F Lewis (Publishers) Ltd, 1934.
Thompson, M, *Woven in Kidderminster 1735–2000*, David Voice Associates, 2002.

Cotton industry

Aspin, C, *Lancashire The First Industrial Society*, Helmshore Local History Society, 1969.
Aspin, C, *The Water Spinners*, Helmshore Local History Society, 2003.
Aspin, C, *The Cotton Industry*, Shire Publications, 2004 reprint.
Burton, A, *The Rise and Fall of King Cotton*, BBC Books, 1984.
Chapman, S D, *The Cotton Industry in the Industrial Revolution*, Macmillan, 1972.
Edwards, Michael M, *The Growth of the British Cotton Trade 1780–1815*,

Manchester University Press, 1967.

Farnie, D A, *The English Cotton Industry and the World Market 1815–1896,* Clarendon Press, 1979.

Frangopulo, N J, *Tradition in Action – The Historical Evolution of the Greater Manchester County,* E P Publishing Ltd, 1977.

Howe, A, *The Cotton Masters,* Clarendon Press, 1984.

Ingle, G, *Yorkshire Cotton,* Carnegie Publishing, 1997.

Longmate, N, *The Hungry Mills,* Temple Smith, London, 1978.

Lowe, N, *The Lancashire Textile Industry in the Sixteenth Century,* Chetham Society, 1972.

Robson, R, *The Cotton Industry in Britain,* Macmillan, 1858, reprint 1957.

General

The Century's Progress: Yorkshire Industry and Commerce 1893, Brenton Publishing, 1893, reprint 1971.

Armstrong, J and Jones, S, *Business Documents: Their origin, sources and uses in historical research,* Mansell, 1987.

Benson, A, *Textile Machines,* Shire Publications, 1983.

Benson, A, and Warburton, N, *Looms and Weaving,* Shire Publications, 2002 reprint.

Berg, M, *The Age of Manufacturers 1700–1820,* Routledge, 1994.

Bond, M F, *Guide to the Records of Parliament,* HMSO, 1971.

Briscoe, L, *The Textile and Clothing Industry of the UK,* Manchester University Press, 1971.

Brooks, P, *How to Research Local History,* Howtobooks, 2006.

Brown, J, *The English Market Town,* Crowood Press, 1986.

Buchanan, R A, *Industrial Archaeology in Britain,* Viking, 1980.

Burn, J S, *The History of the French, Walloon, Dutch and Other Foreign Protestant Refugees Settled in England from the Reign of Henry VIII to the Revocation of the Edict of Nantes,* Longman, Brown, Green and Longman, 1846.

Calladine, A and Fricker, J, *East Cheshire Textile Mills,* RHCME/London, 1993.

Chambers, J D, *The Workshop of the World, British Economic History from 1820–1880,* Oxford University Press, 1967.

Chambers, P, *Early Modern Genealogy,* Sutton Publishing, 2006.

Chambers, P, *Medieval Genealogy,* Sutton Publishing, 2006.

Chapman, S D, *The Beginnings of Industrial Britain,* University Tutorial Press Limited, 1970.

Coleman, D C, *The Economy of England 1450–1750,* Oxford University Press, 1977.

Cunliffe, B (ed.), *England's Landscape: The West,* English Heritage, 2006.

Currer-Briggs, N and Gambier, R, *Huguenot Ancestry,* Phillimore & Co. Ltd, 2001.

Davies, J, *A History of Wales,* Penguin, 1993.

Defoe, D, edited by P Rodgers, *Tour Through the Whole Island of Great Britain,* Penguin Classics, 1724–1727, 1978 reprint.

Derry, T K and Blakeway, M G, *The Making of Early and Medieval Britain,* John Murray, 1968.

English, W, *The Textile Industry,* Longmans, Green & Co. Ltd, 1969.

Giles, C and Goodall, I H, *Yorkshire Textile Mills 1770–1930,* HMSO, 1992.

Gillett, E and MacMahon, K A, *A History of Hull,* Hull University Press, 1980.

Hey, D, *Yorkshire From AD1000,* Longman, 1986.

Hobsbawm, E J, *Industry and Empire,* Penguin Books, 1969.

Hooke, D, *England's Landscape – The West Midlands,* Archibald, 2006.

Hudson, P, *The Genesis of Industrial Capital,* Cambridge University Press, 1986.

Jenkins, D (ed.), *The Cambridge History of Western Textiles,* Cambridge University Press, 2003.

Jeremy, D J, *A Business History of Britain 1900–1990,* Oxford University Press, 1998.

Kershaw, R and Pearsall, M, *Immigrants and Aliens: A guide to sources on UK Immigration and Citizenship,* The National Archives, 2001.

Kirk, R E G, *Returns of Aliens in London, 1523–1603,* Vol X in 4 parts, Huguenot Society, 1900–1908.

McCord, N, *North East England – The Region's Devlopment 1760–1960,* Batsford Academic, 1979.

Orbell, J, *A Guide to Tracing the History of a Business,* Business Archives Council, 1987.

Pilbeam, A, *The Landscape of Gloucestershire,* Tempus, 2006.

Porter, S, *Exploring Urban History,* Batsford Ltd, 1990.

Probert, E, *Company and Business Records for Family Historians,* FFHS, 1994.

Rowlands, J, et al. (eds), *Welsh Family History,* Association of Family History Societies in Wales, 1993.

Rowlands, M B, *The West Midlands from AD 1000,* Longman, 1987.

Sheppard, F, *London – A History,* Oxford University Press, 1998.

Short, B, *England's Landscape – The South East,* Collins, 2006.

Southampton University Industrial Archaeology Group, *Water and Wind Mills in Hampshire and the Isle of Wight,* Southampton University Industrial Archaeology Group, 1978.

Stephens, W B, *Sources for English Local History,* Cambridge University Press, 1981.

Stocker, D, *The East Midlands,* Archibald, 2006.

Williamson, T, *England's Landscape – East Anglia,* Collins, 2006.

Lace industry

Bury Palliser, Mrs, *History of Lace,* Dover Publications Inc, 1901.

Felkin, William, *History of the Machine-wrought Hosiery and Lace Manufactories,* David & Charles Ltd, 1967.

Harte, N B and Ponting, K G (eds), *Textile History and Economic History: Essays in Honour of Miss Julia de Lacy Mann*, Manchester University Press, 1973.

Yallop, H J, *The History of the Honiton Lace Industry*, University of Exeter Press, 1992.

Linen industry

The North Riding Linen Industry, North Yorkshire Archives publication, n.d.

Baines, P, *Flax and Linen*, Shire Publications, 1998 reprint.

Rimmer, W G, *Marshall's of Leeds: Flaxspinners 1788–1886*, Cambridge University Press, 1960.

Roberts, Elizabeth (ed.), *A History of Linen in the North West*, Centre for North West Regional Studies, 1998.

Searle, A G and Tuck, J W, *The King's Flax and the Queen's Linen*, The Larks Press, n.d.

Warden, A J, *The Linen Trade*, F Cass, 1967.

Rope

Sanctuary, A, *Rope, Twine and Net Making*, Shire Publications, 1988 second edn.

Silk Industry

Feltwell, Dr J, *The Story of Silk*, Sutton Publishing, 1990.

Godden, Geoffrey A, *Stevengraphs and Other Victorian Silk Pictures*, Fairleigh Dickinson University Press, 1971.

Warner, F, *The Silk Industry of the UK*, Drane's, 1921.

Wool industry

Aspin, C, *The Woollen Industry*, Shire Publications, 2006 reprint.

Beresford, M, *East End, West End: The Face of Leeds during Urbanisation 1684–1842*, The Thoresby Society, 1988.

Brearley, A and Iredale, J A, *The Woollen Industry*, WIRA, 1965.

Clapham, J H, *Woollen and Worsted Industries*, Pitman & Sons, 1947.

Dumville, J and Kershaw, S, *Worsted Industry*, Pitman & Sons, 1947.

Firth, G, *Bradford and the Industrial Revolution*, Ryburn Publications, 1990.

Heaton, H, *Yorkshire Woollen and Worsted Industries*, Clarendon Press, 1965.

Hind, J R, *Woollen and Worsted Raw Materials*, Ernest Benn Ltd, 1948.

Jenkins, D T and Ponting, K G, *The British Wool Textile Industry 1770–1914*, Heinemann Educational Books, 1982.

Jenkins, J G, *The Welsh Woollen Industry*, National Museum of Wales/Welsh Folk Museum, 1969.

Jubb, S, *The History of the Shoddy Trade: its rise, progress and present position*, Houlson & Wright, 1860.

Keighley, M, *A Fabric Huge – The Story of Listers*, James & James, 1989.
Lipson, E, *The History of the Woollen and Worsted Industries*, F Cass, 1965.
Ponting, K G, *Wool Trade: past and present*, Columbine, 1961.
Ponting, K G, *The Woollen Industry of South-West England*, Adams & Dart, 1971.
Sutton, A, *The Textiles of Wales*, Bellew Publishing Company, 1987.
White, Walter, *A Month in Yorkshire*, M T D Rigg Publications, 1858, reprint 1991.

Fire insurance

Hawkings, D T, *Fire Insurance Records for Family and Local Historians*, Francis Boutle, 2003.
O'Neill, J, 'Fire Insurance Records', *Ancestors*, June 2008

Websites

• www.sheepcentre.co.uk/wool.htm

• www.clothworkers.co.uk/index.php?page=18

• www.leedstrinity.ac.uk/histcourse/suffrage/document/suffhisa.htm

• www.british-history.ac.uk/Default.aspx – British History Online is the digital library containing some of the core printed primary and secondary sources for the medieval and modern history of the British Isles. Created by the Institute of Historical Research and the History of Parliament Trust, the organisation aims to support academic and personal users around the world in their learning, teaching and research.

• www.nnwfhs.org.uk/publications/journals/H2.pdf – Judy Vero, 'Hatting', *Atherstone, Nuneaton & North Warwickshire Family History Society Journal*.

• www.ehs.org.uk/ehs/conference2007/Assets/HoneymanIIB.doc – relates to London apprentices and where they went to.

• www.galaxy.bedfordshire.gov.uk/webingres/luton/0.local/hat_industry.htm – history of the Bedfordshire hat industry.

• www.rootsweb.com/~engbdf/lace.html – history of Bedfordshire lace.

• www.leicesterchronicler.com/corah.htm – information about the history of the textile firm Corah Ltd.

INDEX